Bernd-Ulrich Kaiser

Corporate Information with SAP®-EIS

Efficient Business Computing

Edited by Stephen Fedtke

This series of books covers special topics which are useful for project managers, team leaders, and businessmen involved in data processing. These books impart how new technologies may be profitable for business. The practical knowhow presented in this series comes from the authors' countless years of experience in business computing. Specifically, these books will help you to:
- use new technologies as well as future-oriented strategies
- reduce costs and exploit the potential of the market
- improve the productivity of business companies
- implement the basis of precise decisions and put these into practice for the management
- ensure competent support for business projects and data processing
- reduce training time and cost.

These books are practical guides from experts for experts. Those who read these books today will surely benefit from their knowledge tomorrow.

The editor, Dr. Stephen Fedtke, is software developer, consultant and book author. He is also editor of the series of books called "Efficient Software-Development" also published by the Vieweg Verlag, of which many books are successfully published.

Books already in print:

QM-Optimizing der Softwareentwicklung
QM-Handbuch gemäß DIN ISO 9001 und
Leitfaden für best practices im Unternehmen
von Dieter Burgartz und Thomas Blum

Client/Server-Architektur
von Klaus D. Niemann

DV-Revision
Ordnungsmäßigkeit, Sicherheit und Wirtschaftlichkeit von DV-Systemen
von Jürgen de Haas und Sixta Zerlauth

Chipkarten-Systeme erfolgreich realisieren
Das umfassende, aktuelle Handbuch
von Monika Klieber

Telearbeit erfolgreich realisieren
Das umfassende, aktuelle Handbuch
von Norbert Kordey und Werner B. Korte

Unternehmensinformation mit SAP®-EIS
Aufbau eines Data Warehouse und einer inSight®-Anwendung
von Bernd-Ulrich Kaiser

Unternehmesweites Datenmanagement
von Klaus Schwinn, Rolf Dippold, André Ringgenberg
und Walter Schnider

Corporate Information with SAP®-EIS
Building a Data Warehouse and a MIS-Application with inSight®
by Bernd-Ulrich Kaiser

Vieweg

Bernd-Ulrich Kaiser

Corporate Information with SAP®-EIS

Building a Data Warehouse and a
MIS-Application with inSight®

Edited by Stephen Fedtke

GABLER vieweg

Originally published in the German language by Friedr. Vieweg & Sohn Verlagsgesellschaft mbH, D-65189 Wiesbaden, Germany under the title 'Unternehmensinformation mit SAP®-EIS, 2. Auflage (2nd Edition)
© Friedr. Vieweg & Sohn Verlagsgesellschaft mbH, Braunschweig/Wiesbaden, 1998

1st Edition 1998

Vieweg is a subsidiary company of Bertelsmann Professional Information.

Printing and binding: Lengericher Druckerei Hubert & Co., Göttingen
Printed on acid-free paper
Printed in Germany

ISBN 3-528-05674-6

Forward

There is no doubt that the rapid developments in the field of information technology have had and will continue to have a profound influence on the way we lead our lives. Whether or not we have reached the stage of an "information society" is a question that can not yet be answered.

Upon closer examination, one can see a rift developing in the corporate world. In addition to the euphoria of users who have embraced and mastered these new technologies, there is also bitterness and fear among employees who have not made the leap to "computer literacy." Despite the lofty promises found in product advertising materials, the point has not yet been reached where these new attention-catching systems can be intuitively operated with little or no training.

While developments in information technology threaten the job security of analysts and junior managers who fall behind the curve, the prestige and power of senior managers protect them from similar consequences. Unfortunately, it is usually the company as a whole that suffers when, regardless of the cause, management is reluctant or slow to embrace emerging technologies.

On the other hand, managers reasonably expect information technology to help them with their daily decision-making process, instead of simply being an additional brain-teasing responsibility. They desire a quick and comprehensive overview of important information, without having to sacrifice much of their valuable time. Managers are not interested in hearing about technical inadequacies, they expect results.

It can not be stressed enough, how important upper management support is to the development of a system. A manager who develops a vision for a corporate management information system, and is able to convince the board of directors to support the project, is crucial to the long-term success of a system.

These are the conditions and situation that encouraged a "technology foreigner" to accept the challenge of corporate information needs, and to move from being a chemist (in research, production, and management) to developing a functional information system.

One quickly realizes that nobody seems to be interested in the problems associated with developing an information system: the combined marketing efforts of hardware manufactures, software vendors, and consultants have convinced the corporate world that these problems are all minor in scale. The system developer is then left to bridge the gap between what is necessary and what is technically possible.

With the benefit of hindsight, it is clear that this analysis was a valuable experience. Sometimes new ideas and possibilities are like wild animals that need to be tamed. That can only be accomplished by a team, with representatives from various business areas and industries. One quickly recognizes that data processing technology alone is no guarantee for building and implementing a successful system.

With this in mind, I would like to thank all those who supported, accompanied, or tolerated me along this journey.

The concepts addressed in this book are the result of all the combined efforts that went into building and maintaining a management information system at Bayer. The system has been running under the name ISOM (Information System for Operative Management) since the end of 1993.

In particular, I would like to thank Mr. Münch, who shaped the development of the system from the very beginning, as well as Erich Breitschwerdt and Udo Wollschläger, whose input through numerous conceptual and technical discussions was immense. I would also like to thank Claudia Blumberg, Gudrun Beck, Michaela Hinz and Jürgen Vermum for their critiques and comments related to the manuscript.

Leverkusen, June 1998

Bernd-Ulrich Kaiser

Contents

1 Introduction

1.1   Goal of the Book

New MIS Techniques

The building of successful Management Information Systems (MIS) is often plagued by resistance from the target group. Traditional data processing strategies are not always appropriate for MIS development. New processes are based on ideas like Data Warehousing, OLAP (On-Line Analytical Processing), and Data Mining. The trick lies in using these new technologies to build a system that is compatible with and exploits the existing corporate data processing infrastructure and standards.

SAP®-EIS, inSight®

This book describes a proven method for developing and operating a successful MIS, using a relational database (more specifically, the Executive Information System from SAP, SAP®-EIS), with the user interface program inSight® (from arcplan). It shows effective means for determining information needs, achieving high-quality information input and output, building a Data Warehouse, and designing an end-user interface. It also examines methodologies for incorporating new Internet technologies into an MIS.

System Users

Such systems are generally designed for computer illiterate managers who are reluctant to learn how to use complex or complicated applications. Therefore, the focus of the system must be the display of relevant and useful corporate information (i.e. sales data, cost analyses, etc.). Through a flexible, modular system architecture, the system is able to provide an excellent price-performance ratio.

Collection of Ideas

The variety and complexity of real corporate operations make it impossible to define an exact plan for building an information system. However, it is possible to use examples to demonstrate general situations common to many firms. The exact plan an individual company will follow depends on the system goals and the resources available to the system design team. In this sense, this book is a collection of suggestions and ideas based on the

1

experiences of developing and maintaining a corporate-wide MIS at a large German company.

1.2 Terminology

The following is not simply a list of commonly-used marketing definitions, but rather a critical examination of technical terms as they relate to building an MIS.

1.2.1 Data Warehouse (DWH)

In recent years, it seems that no data processing phrase has been used as often and as ambiguously as "Data Warehouse." This is probably due to the fact that the concept of a well-stocked warehouse is easy to imagine, but is also open to individual interpretation. As this imagery is both positive and encouraging, the concept of a Data Warehouse quickly established itself as the symbolic goal of many companies.

A key reason for the popularity of the DWH concept (in which the user is able to easily access data stored on the server) was ECKERSON's 1993 definition of the term:

ECKERSON wrote that data warehousing was a process of extraction and consolidation of data stored in different sources to be put into a decision support database which is easily accessed by the user and offers comfortable search possibilities.[1]

Catch .22 DWH-MIS

In practice, this process is not so easy to achieve. It is often difficult to find the resources necessary to build a complex DWH without support and input from MIS users. Conversely, it is almost impossible to develop an MIS without simultaneously building a DWH. Coordinating these two processes takes a great deal of patience, communication, and trust. Many conceptually excellent projects have failed because this coordination was not achieved.

1.2.2 Data Marts

Intentional Redundancy

A "Data Mart" displays an intentionally redundant section of the corporate Data Warehouse. Data marts are generally custom-designed for specific user groups, and contain information like sales and cost figures for a given region, a given product group, or a given time range.[2]

In this sense, a data mart is really just a smaller Data Warehouse. The concept of a data mart became popular when larger firms realized the difficulties involved in developing corporate-wide Data Warehouses. Concepts like data marts grew out of frustrations in creating MIS, and to keep the idea of an MIS alive and attractive in firms that experienced failures or setbacks in Data Warehouse design.

1.2.3 Information Systems

1.2.3.1 Information Systems for Management

The Definition of Information Systems Often Falls on a Theoretical Level

HABERLANDT was one of the first to define the term "Management Information System". He defined it as "the totality of per ₁nnel, materials, and organizational structures used by a firm for data and information processing. "[3]

This purely business-oriented formulation makes it clear that information systems consist of more than just electronic data processing, "even though this is frequently the most important tool used. "[4]

Technical developments in the field of EDP have opened new dimensions for rationally processing large data sets. In most firms today, EDP is the base from which efficient information systems are developed. Since this book deals exclusively with computer-supported information systems, it makes sense to consider MEYER's definition:

A "computer-supported information system" is a system "in which the collection, storage, transmission, and/or transformation of information is in part automated through the use of EDP. "[5]

BULLINGER formulated an interesting corollary to Meyer with regards to the current state of Leadership Information Systems (LIS):

Leadership Culture

"LIS are a part of leadership culture. They can't be limited to individual issues or concerns, but instead must be integrated into the entire organization. "[6]

The term "Information System" is used as a stand-alone definition, but is also often combined with other terms to create specialized or customized definitions. Some of these customized definitions are listed below, although it should be noted that trying to differentiate some of these "hyphenated" terms from each other is often pointless or even impossible.

Preparing Leadership Information

An "Executive Information System" (EIS) is understood to be an information system for a "boss, senior executive, or board member." An EIS is designed to "provide corporate leaders with direct access to internal and external data that are critical to the success of the firm. "[7]

"Management Information Systems" [8] (MIS) were born out of the need to create "systems to provide leadership information." In this sense they are virtually identical to EIS, so there is no need to draw any further distinctions between these two terms.

So-called "Decision Support Systems" (DSS) are designed with a different goal in mind. DSS are defined as "dialog systems with a decision model to aid the decision-making process of corporate leaders."[9] DSS are prevalent and helpful in companies with poorly structured data and information systems.

SCHEER identified the essential characteristics of a DSS as being "high interactivity," "flexible [stand-alone, the author] modeling capabilities for the end-user," "a short learning cycle so that it [the system, the author] can embed itself in the decision process of the user" and "an emphasis on quick information access over mathematical optimization."[10]

Operative systems - or administrative systems, as MERTENS and GRIESE call them[11] - should be thought of as "order processing" systems in the broadest sense of the term, although their main goal is to "integrate massive data processing into the administration."[12] In this book, the term "Base System" is synonymous with "Operative System" (not to be confused with "Operative Information System," see page 6).

The Multitude of Software Products for MIS

Many attempts have been made to build functional information systems based on the IS variations that have been discussed so far. Such attempts may sound impressive in internal and external press releases, but overall they have a minimal impact on corporate reporting quality. This problem is exacerbated by software companies; they find it easier to develop programs aimed at specific IS segments, rather than to develop a program to meet the entire spectrum of modern corporate reporting needs.

Corporate Information

In the modern corporation, information from various sources and systems is constantly flowing back and forth. It is hard to imagine that a manager would accept and work with all these different systems on his personal computer. Of course, different managers have different information needs. A strategic planner's information needs will differ from those of an operative manager, even if they are working on the same project. The key is to develop a single system that can provide multiple perspectives of corporate data, rather than developing a series of inter-dependent systems that each offer a single perspective of the data.

Supporting the Manager

A management information system should support managers. Therefore, it should be able to access and process data from all the corporate areas with which a manager has contact. Using the technology available today, it is difficult to quickly develop such a system (and to be sure that it will operate without bugs or problems). This needs to be the goal, however, or a company is likely to end up with a number of unrelated or incompatible systems all processing the same data.

The importance of MIS (also sometimes called "Strategic Information Systems," or SIS) to a manager is clear. The importance of "Operative Information Systems" (OIS) must also be considered.

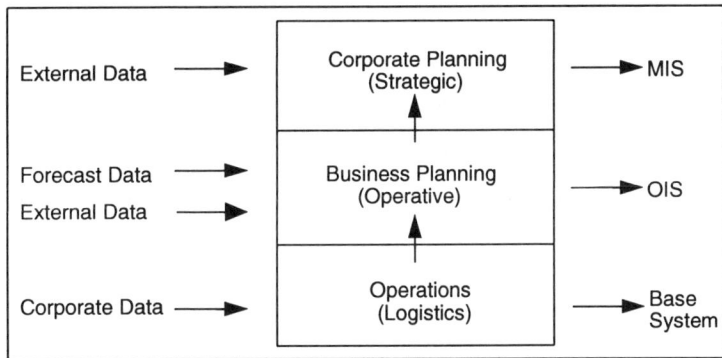

Exhibit 1: Information Structure

1.2.3.2

Standard Software

Operative Information Systems (OIS)

Every large corporation today runs a number of EDP programs, all designed to support the technical administration of corporate data. From the classic personnel systems, to the logistic programs, and on to day-to-day business applications, companies rely on stable, dependable software. These EDP applications, often referred to as base systems, were in large part responsible for the data processing successes of the '60's and '70's. The trend now is moving to standard software, most notably SAP, which provides benefits above and beyond those possible with custom-designed applications.

The whole process becomes murkier when so-called "Operative Information Systems" are considered. The reasoning for such systems is that a manager needs access to all the base information relating to his department or project, regardless of where that data is stored. The existing EDP structure in most companies does not allow for easy interaction between different base systems.

Management and strategic information systems, on the other hand, are reliant on consolidated information. These systems process consolidated data and display key business figures (% variation from plan, comparison to last year, etc.) in graphic and/or report form.

Typical MIS Information:	Product A Results for Region B		
Result for Month XY:	200 (8 % From Sales)		
Variation from Budget:	+ 6	+ 3 %	
Variation from Previous Year	+12	+ 6	----> Graphic Display
Typical OIS Information:	Customer C Profile		
Last Visit:	3.5.96 (Visit Report)		
Contact Person:	Smith, Wilson		
Budget 96:	...		
Contracts 96:	---> Products, Quantities, Prices, Conditions		
Open Contracts:	---> Delivery Dates, Status, Inventory		
Open Payables:	---> Payments		
Complaints:	Due Incidents		
Status of Projects:	---> Projects		
Credit Line:	...		

Exhibit 2: Information Systems - MIS/OIS Differences

The difference between an MIS and an OIS can also be seen in their different application areas within business reporting systems. The decisive distinction is that OIS are fed information from accounting and business analysis systems, while MIS draw data from strategic systems.

Accounting Systems	Legal Entity-Oriented Calculation
Controlling Systems	Business Unit-Oriented Perspective
• Business Analysis Systems	Customer/Product-Oriented Perspective
• Strategy Systems	Corporation/Market-Oriented Perspective
OIS	Integrating the Relevant Aspects from Accounting and Business Analysis
MIS	Integrating the Relevant Aspects from Managerial Strategy

Exhibit 3: Business-Oriented Reporting Systems

1.2.4   Information Broker

Information Acquisition

Similar to a Data Warehouse, the concept of an "Information Broker" arose from the realization that providing management with adequate amounts of timely, reliable data within justifiable economic constraints was almost impossible with the then-available technologies.[13] Information brokers are, unlike Data Warehouses, typically used to collect and evaluate data from external sources. It makes sense, however, to develop a similar system for providing management with data from internal corporate sources as (see page 191).

1.2.5   OLAP

Multidimensional Approach

"OLAP stands for 'On-Line Analytical Processing' In contrast to the more familiar OLTP ('On-Line Transaction Processing'), OLAP describes a class of technologies that are designed for live *ad hoc* data access and analysis. While transaction processing generally relies solely on relational databases, OLAP has become synonymous with *multidimensional* views of business data. These multidimensional views are supported by multidimensional database technology. These multidimensional views provide the technical basis for the calculations and analysis required by Business Intelligence applications. "[14]

As E. F. CODD, the father of the relational data model, wrote in 1993, "(...) they are limited in their ability to present data in

7

different formats, under different headings and according to diverse dimensions. "[15]

OLAP offers users a multidimensional view of data, in the form of "hyper cubes." This makes it possible to do analyses over every possible dimension of the data.[16]

1.2.6   Data Mining

Data Mining
Automatically Finds
Relationships

"Data Mining" is a term used to describe a system that automatically registers important but unnoticed irregularities or deviations in large data sets. A properly-functioning data mining system can detect financially beneficial opportunities or existing resource-draining investments, allowing a company to identify and exploit trends that would otherwise remain undetected.

Corporations produce and store huge amounts of data relating to daily operations. The US retail chain Wal-Mart alone generates over 20 million data records per day. Even mid-size companies record several hundred thousand data entries in a typical month. It is difficult for a company to sift through these mounds of data and filter out truly important information.

Traditional analysis methods have proven to be too passive. If the user isn't completely familiar with the data behind the analysis, critical assumptions must be made. The danger that these assumptions are incorrect, or that the user simply fails to recognize important logical relationships, is too high for a modern corporation to risk.

Data mining is designed to eliminate such dangers from corporate reporting systems. It automatically generates logical assumptions, checks these against relevant patterns, and presents the results to the user in an easy-to-understand form.

The theory implications of data mining are quite intriguing from a scientific standpoint: From a pure business perspective, the emphasis must be on clearly achievable and identifiable benefits. Although some existing systems have shown considerable promise, more extensive systems need to be built and analyzed before data mining can be considered an essential corporate analysis tool.[17]

1.2.7   Internet/Intranet

Technology Prod -
Internet

The Internet is a world-wide connection of different networks, allowing computers from all over the world to link and exchange data. The Internet is the world's largest data network, and is theoretically accessible by each and every PC user.

Individual networks within the Internet are independently administered by various organizations. Although some of these organizations perform operations important for all Internet users, there is no one agency or organization responsible for the Internet as a whole. The most important consequences of the Internet's informal structure, from an information system point of view, are:

- There is no guarantee that a given service or server in the Internet is always accessible
- No system has yet been developed that can guarantee the confidentiality and integrity of data transmitted over the Internet

Innovation HTML

After 20 years of use mainly by Internet specialists, the World Wide Web (WWW) has emerged as the most popular Internet information service. Based largely on the HTML (Hyper Text Markup Language) programming language, the WWW has caused use of and interest in the Internet to explode over the last three years.

HTML offered completely new possibilities, and quickly established itself as the secret Internet standard. HTML's strengths are as follows:

- Extremely user-friendly interface (FUN)
- "Hyperlink" possibilities
- Processing of unstructured information
- Ability to be combined with pictures, sound, video etc.
- Platform independent
- Easy to install

Despite its relatively short life to-date, some notable weaknesses in HTML have been identified:

- No dynamic processes
- "One-dimensional"
- Handling of structured data (tables, arrays)
- No data-driven update solutions

One can assume, however, that HTML (in conjunction with the Internet communication protocol TCP/IP) will significantly influence future data processing strategies. As an example, it is hard to imagine an information system in the near future that will not include built-in HTML capabilities.

2   Information Supply and Information Quality

2.1   Information Supply

2.1.1   Structured Information

Classical information systems concentrate on the numeric data used in business reports and balance sheets. The drill-down technique, whereby a user moves from a consolidated data entry directly to the individual data records comprising the consolidated entry, was designed to give insights into corporate and industry developments. A manager should thus be able to identify specific actions that need to be or should be taken.

Corporate Data

Base information usually consists of numeric data in the form of a multidimensional data cube. For example, a user may want to compare turnover, costs, and gross profit against competitors' results based on products, customers, and a selected time range. The numeric data of the individual dimensions can be consolidated at a number of different levels, with the end result being the results for the entire corporation.

Such a data collection can be very large and very complex. Considering the time dimension alone, the decision must be made whether or not to correct older data when new data becomes available. For example, how should a system handle an incorrect entry from a previous month that is corrected by a new entry in the current month? Some reports only make corrections on a quarterly basis. As a result, the individual monthly figures, when added together, will not necessarily result in the same total as the quarterly report.

If structured information is to be used in an information system, a Data Warehouse architecture is necessary. This is the only data design that allows for an effective controlling of information quality. Whether this should be a corporate-wide, open Data Warehouse, or a Data Warehouse used exclusively by the information system, is a question that is addressed elsewhere in this book (page 29).

Structured data has the reputation of being good quality data. Its value for later analyses, however, must be constantly reevaluated. When possible, the data itself and the structure of the data should be improved.

2.1.2 Unstructured Information

Search Systems

The simplest examples of unstructured information are formatted text information, graphs, and pictures. In comparison to structured information, the contents of unstructured information can't be easily categorized in a database table. A query language comparable to SQL is missing. Thus the justification for search systems, which search the entire table for terms, word strings, or word combinations. Even search systems that operate on the basis of key terms enjoy widespread acceptance.

Object-Oriented Databases

There are modern database systems that offer additional features for storing and finding unstructured information. First, an information object is defined. This object can then be stored in the database as a so-called BLOB (binary large object). The object description can be stored relationally. The result is a performance-oriented database architecture capable of administering and navigating through the entire database.

This technique has not found wide-spread acceptance in the field of management information systems. Few vendors of MIS systems recognize unstructured information to be of critical importance. This is also true for SAP®-EIS; text information like conference minutes can not (yet) be flexibly incorporated into end user models. In the face of developing Internet technologies, where texts are easily processed and accessed, ignoring the importance of unstructured data appears to directly conflict with the future needs of end users.

It is difficult to control the quality of unstructured data, because the ability to process BLOBs with existing data manipulation language tools is limited.

2.1.3 Current Data

Information Today Must be Up-to-Date

To gain acceptance and survive, an information system must reflect up-to-date data. Large firms in particular have developed mechanisms to insure that current data is quickly available where it needs to be available. The expense and effort needed to insure up-to-date data seems to be unimportant. The expanse of information vehicles includes personal couriers, various mailing possibilities, and faxing. Of course, nobody wants to give up these comforts just for the sake of installing an MIS. On the other hand, one of the goals of an MIS should be to replace the existing sub-optimal information transfer systems.

Therefore, it is of crucial importance that an MIS provide current, up-to-date information.

New information should be sent out, not retrieved. This belief has become ingrained in many corporate cultures, to the point that any other type of information system is unimaginable. Armies of secretaries and assistants insure daily that new data is "provided" to analysts and management.

Drilldown Technique Based on "Retrieved" Information

This may seem a trivial point, but a user-driven system will not succeed in a culture geared towards "provided information." Naturally, the culture of the firm will have important consequences on the architecture of an information system. Many software companies stress their advanced drilldown technologies, with which managers can locate the information they want or need. The question is, how willing is an "information-provided" manager going to be to learn and operate a drilldown system? To achieve long-term success, the developer must find a way to incorporate the end user into the application.

Employees often use information strategically to "make an impression" on their bosses. They use the opportunity to express their personal opinions about the information, or to discuss other issues that they consider important. An automatic information system that provides up-to-date information removes this opportunity. For this reason, many employees reject or conspire against such a system, and the people responsible for introducing it. System sponsors and developers should keep this in mind when developing an introduction strategy. They need to find ways to convince all employees that the new information concept is valid and beneficial to them and the company (see also page 105).

2.1.4   Depth of Detail

Don't Show All the Data!

Only at first glance does it seem beneficial to use an information system to access all the data in a Data Warehouse. There are

13

many reasons why such an undertaking is an expensive proposition.

Some industry publications suggest, in the quest for a perfect information system, that the end user should have full access to all the data in the Data Warehouse, as well as access to the base data from operative systems. This is in direct contrast to the true logic behind an information system. In reality, a company must be very careful in selecting what data is appropriate for a management information system, and should not provide access to all data just because it is technically accessible.

A monthly reporting system for an international corporation will serve as an example. The related data cube consists of seven dimensions:

	-------------------- Consolidation Levels ---------------------			
Dimensions	0	1	2	3
1. Deliverer	Company	Country	Region	all Deliverer
2. Receiver	Company	Country	Region	all Receiver
3. Product	BU	FoB	FoW	all Products
4. Position				
5. Time				
6. Budgetary State				
7. Currency				
Comm.: Company = Entity within a Corporation, BU = Business Unit, FoB = Field of Business, FoW = Field of Work				

Exhibit 4: Business Report Structures

Examples for:

- **Balance Sheet Item**: Turnover, Profit
- **Time**: Month, Cumulative Month
- **State**: Current Year Actual, Previous Year Actual, Budget, Revised Budget
- **Currency**: DM, Local Currency.

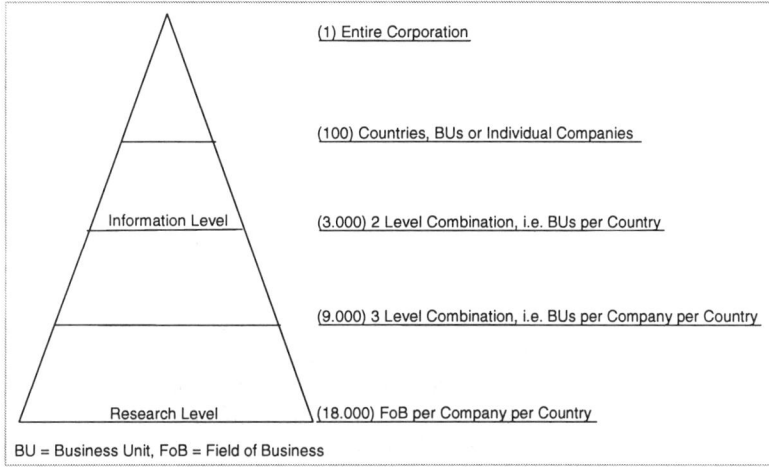

Exhibit 5: Consolidation Levels

18.000 Data Records The corporate sum in this reporting system is based on approximately 18,000 individual data records. The hierarchical levels that build up to the corporate sum can be categorized into distinct information levels.

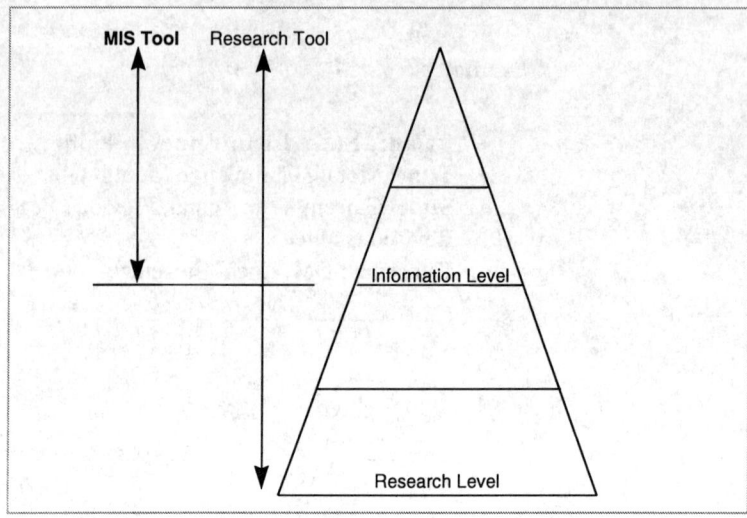

Exhibit 6: Data Processing Tools

Different Tools

The information level is placed in the middle of the pyramid. This is the data area where the user of a management information system can move to via the drill-down technique. The two levels below the information level contain mathematical calculations used for controlling and analysis by analysts. Using the same data processing technology, these analysts can be provided with various research tools to aid them in their work (see also page 138).

Better Quality Data, Easier Research

Drawing this distinction has a number of advantages. First, only the data beginning with the information level must have the guaranteed accuracy needed for information system analyses by top management. Data below the information level is only accessed by analysts and controllers, whose detailed knowledge of their specific fields makes it possible for them to recognize and evaluate implausible data variations.

If a top manager has a question regarding data at the information level, an employee with access to the entire corporate data structure (but at a research level) can most easily and economically find the answer. This is not possible when a top manager has access to and a question related to research level data. This often leads to extensive research and work, often times by employees in other divisions or even other subsidiaries. The hidden costs of data acquisition rise tremendously in such a case. Many high-level managers have confirmed that they don't need access to detailed research level information. But if the information is there, these managers are likely to look at it and develop questions related to it.

2.2   Transaction Systems

2.2.1   SAP Systems

Standard Software

SAP AG offers two software solutions: SAP® R/2 for mainframes and SAP® R/3 for client/server structures. SAP® R/2 and SAP® R/3 feature the following distinguishing characteristics:[18]

- complete business transaction coverage
- modular development
- industry neutral
- clear structuring
- international application

Numerous large corporations world-wide are replacing their in-house developed transaction systems with standard SAP software programs. The goal is better system integration and a long-term reduction in software maintenance costs. The move to SAP systems is often accompanied by reengineering projects. For larger firms, the total costs for software licenses, installations, and training can range from tens of millions to hundreds of millions per year.

At the present time, most firms see no real alternatives to SAP's systems.

From an information system perspective, companies can only benefit from a standard software like SAP: In addition to unifying structures and indexes, it also provides access to information throughout the corporation.

2.2.1.1   SAP® R/2

The (older) SAP® R/2 system was designed for mainframe computers. Some of the transaction modules available in the R/2 system are:

- RV - Sales, Invoicing, Distribution
- RM-PPS - Production Planning and Controlling
- RM-MAT – Materials Management
- RM-QSS - Quality Management

2.2.1.2 SAP® R/3

Since its introduction in 1992, the SAP® R/3 system has become the leading client/server product world-wide. SAP® R/3 can already boast more than 4,000 installations. Already, the 3.0 release of R/3 offers an expanded and improved range of features and functions over those in SAP® R/2.

2.2.2 Other Systems

Despite the incredible success enjoyed by SAP, the better part of "daily business" transactions are still done by in-house developed base systems. Programmed mostly in COBOL, these older applications tend to be rather complex and idiosyncratic. The reason for this can be traced back to the programmers themselves, who often had to resort to unconventional methods to guarantee acceptable response times on older computers. Today, a major problem is that the "last living expert" is no longer around to explain what tricks were built into the system and why. Making major changes to existing programs is therefore often a risky undertaking.

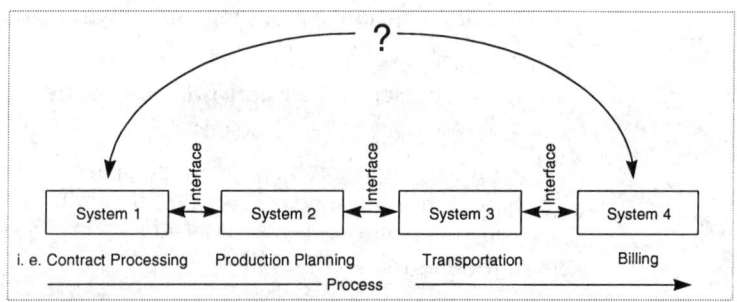

Exhibit 7: Process Chain

The First Doesn't "Understand" the Last

Building an information system based on such transaction systems is a monumental task. Older transaction systems tend to consist of task-specific, independently-developed programs. Communication with other systems in the data processing chain must take place over external interfaces (as a replacement for the missing integration that would be provided by universal yet targeted data structures). Many help programs convert key data in such a way that they can only be understood and processed by the specific system that is next in the data processing chain.

2.3   Expert Information Systems

2.3.1   Financial Results

Result Reporting Systems Not Always Optimal

The corporate financial reporting system is one of the most important data sources for an MIS. Such a system usually displays all the positive characteristics of a Data Warehouse: revised, redundancy-free data records, including comparative historical data. Financial results are generally designed for the central finance department and external analysts, not for managerial needs. In light of this, financial results are of limited use as a steering instrument for optimizing business processes. Using financial results as a managerial tool is made even more difficult by different functional calculation methodologies: Production uses a cost accounting system based on actual values, while marketing tends to allocate costs. It is impossible to display the results of these different systems with a single result reporting system, and few companies are willing to maintain and run two or more parallel financial result systems.

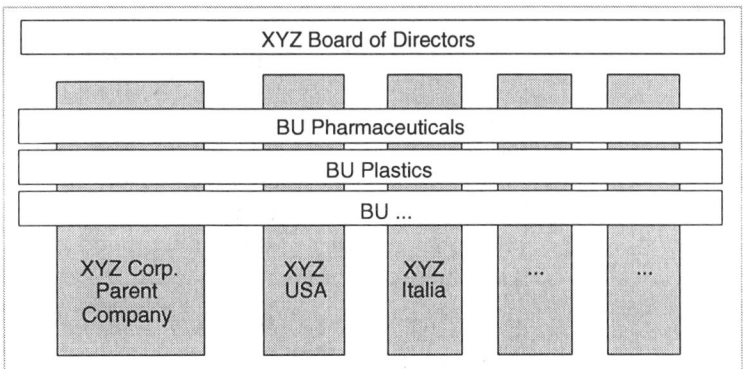

Exhibit 8: Corporate Structure

Missing Consolidations

Another problem arises in larger companies with multiple subsidiaries. The law requires that each "legal entity" report its own separate financial results. This is a legacy of times past when individual businesses were largely independent and selected strategies based on financial reporting results. In response to the globalization of markets, many companies have pushed result responsibility down to the individual business unit level. Unfortunately, this responsibility shift occurred for the most part without a corresponding adjustment in financial result reporting. It is not unusual, therefore, for a corporate-wide consolidation to be missing consolidated results at the product level.

2.3.2   Planning Systems

Different Starting
Points for Planning
Systems

Planning systems include sales planning, purchase planning, production planning, cost planning, profit planning and financial planning, to name a few. Based on the explicit goals of the system, a number of different risks are often ignored or downplayed. Sales planning systems, which are usually more of a sales target, are often very optimistic. A normal sales planning system isn't capable of building in "what if" scenarios to develop a truly realistic plan. Cost planning systems are often similarly optimistic. If figures from both the sales and cost planning systems are used to feed profit planning and financial planning systems, the likelihood of higher than reasonable profit expectations is high.

The practice of manually planning risk into a hierarchical structure is, despite its necessity, usually an arbitrary process.

2.3.3   Controlling Systems

Data Usefulness

Data from base level processing systems can be used to feed data into MIS systems, but the resulting information is only valuable in so far as it can be interpreted by users familiar with the information and the market. The term "data usefulness" is related to this idea. Data is only useful if it leads system users to the correct conclusion. Data can be "correct" (i.e. free of computational errors), but if it is interpreted incorrectly, it can lead to sometimes dangerous management conclusions.

The terms "correct, " and "coherent" make this distinction clear. When used to interpret figures from business reports, the importance of "coherent" data quickly becomes apparent.

	Correct: Correct According to Bookkeeping Guidelines	Coherent: Coherent within the Display Context
• Accounting Systems	+	
• Controlling Systems		
- Business Analysis Systems		+
- Strategy Systems		+

Exhibit 9: The Difference Between "Correct" and "Coherent"

It is not unusual for controlling employees to adjust ("refine") the data stored in information system databases, or to at least use footnotes to identify and clarify confusing entries.

Basis	Usually the Same Source (Base System Data)
Rules	
• Terminology	Not Always Directly
• Assessment	Justifiable Differences
• Consolidation	Justifiable Differences
• Distribution	Justifiable Differences
Links	Not automatically created

Exhibit 10: Links Between Controlling Systems

All market-oriented reporting systems use the same base system data output as their data source. The data output is usually numeric data that has been processed by the corporate accounting system and the financial result reporting programs.

Controlling Systems Take on Lives of Their Own

The variety of reporting and controlling systems used by a company tend to develop lives of their own, specifically through unique terminologies, calculations, consolidations, and cost accounting methods. The differences from system to system are ground in solid business logic, even if the end results are indecipherable to many in the company. The steps that tie these systems together are usually manual processes, so they don't explain the conversions or logic that was used. It is easy to see how running a myriad of systems can result in different departments or business units supplying different answers to the same question.

A very simple example of terminology problems involves geographic subdivisions. "Europe" is often defined differently in different systems. This is not an issue based solely on political or economic definitions, but rather relates to the business structures of individual firms. In many companies, geographic definitions are different from business unit to business unit, so a single company can face the dilemma of having multiple definitions of a term like "Europe."

Examples of regional analyses

- by geographic regions (single)
- by standard corporate reporting units (single)
- by responsibility (multiple, business unit-driven)
- by economic area (market-driven)
- by integrated structure (supplier-driven)

Exhibit 11: Different Responsibility Structures

2.3.4   Other Corporate Systems

In addition to the "classical" data processing systems for logistic, administration, and controlling, companies usually run other data processing programs that can be used as foundations for an information system. If these other corporate systems are to be used effectively, the information system developer needs to have a good relationship with the data processing department. With the complex and "creative" solutions built into systems by programmers, it is rare that a corporate system has a clean file structure and an easily-recognizable key index. The data processing department is not, however, responsible for the contents of the system. Individual departments are responsible for providing accurate data for the various data processing systems.

With some luck, these other systems may provide important elements for developing an information system. Unfortunately, experience has shown that optimism with regards to these systems should be guarded. "Ready-to-use" systems, which can be seamlessly integrated into an information system, are rare.

2.4   External Information Sources

2.4.1   Online Services

For years, online service providers have belonged to the leaders of electronic information distributors. Information available includes stock market information, economic indicator data, and up-to-date news headlines. The quality of the information is extremely high. But there is a problem with online data. Due to the different structures used to provide and process information, an information system that automatically delivers data effectively is a rarity.

End User Interface
Needs
Even if the user base is small, technical issues make it difficult to institute and administer an accepted standard system: No easy-to-use interface exists that is universally recognized by all end users.

Online services have proven to be an excellent source for internal corporate areas like market research, public relations, and finance. These areas themselves then become data providers, feeding their information as base data into corporate-wide information systems.

2.4.2   Internet

At the present time, it is difficult to estimate how useful the Internet will become as a basis for developing management information systems. When one considers Internet technology, it is almost certain that all online services will soon be using the same technology. The Internet is widely perceived as a provider of free information that can be accessed world-wide. To elaborate on this definition, the majority of the information available is advertising-related or promotional by nature, and generally provides little true information "value."

Some software companies have developed interesting Internet products. Pointcast is one of them. Pointcast is able to "magically" display the latest and most up-to-date news on a user's screen. The question is whether or not there will prove to be a broad market for such products.

2.4.3   Other External Information Sources

In addition to data sources within a data network, data and texts can be purchased in electronic form or on paper from institutes, publishing houses, consultants, etc. Due to the variety of formats used by these organizations (most of which are protected against data extraction), these sources should be regarded at best as secondary providers of data for information systems.

3 Data Warehouse

3.1 Requirements

3.1.1 Content and Concept Requirements

Understanding Correct <u>and</u> Coherent Data

What content and technical demands should a Data Warehouse fulfill? First, a distinction needs to be made between **correct and coherent data** (see page 21). Correct data is data that accurately portrays numeric information, but does not necessarily lead a viewer to the appropriate conclusion for a given company or market situation. Using "correct" data to make historical comparisons can be dangerous as well. "Coherent" data, on the other hand, provides the user with the proper business perspective for drawing conclusions and making decisions. A system that completely replaced "correct" data with "coherent" data would be a less than optimal system. A Data Warehouse needs to store both types of data. The MIS application decides what is displayed on the monitor (usually choosing "coherent" data over "correct" data).

A Data Warehouse must offer **multiple data perspectives**. The question is whether or not an MIS application can better provide these perspectives. In any case, the data has to be organized so that analysis tools can easily access the data, and that query response times are acceptable.

Mobile Computing versus On-line Access

An important demand today is **location-independent data access**. The proliferation of corporate-wide Intranets confirms this. When accessing data from a hotel during a business trip, "mobile computing" (in which specific data sets are loaded into the laptop before the trip) strategies compete with on-line connections (over the Internet, for example) which enable access to entire corporate data resources. Regardless of the method used, security issues are paramount. If the data is stored on the hard drive of the portable computer, steps must be taken to prevent unauthorized data accesses (if the computer is lost, stolen, or needs to be repaired). On-line connections require a user identification and verification system, to prevent outsiders from accessing the corporate data processing system. Little empirical data exists with regards to the security of wireless connections (like MODACOM, the wireless system of German Telecom).

For a system to run properly, it is essential to have **clearly-defined responsibilities for preparing and controlling data**. The necessary organizational measures for such a system are not always easy to implement and maintain. For a specific application, it is beneficial to have a "Content Manager" and a "Preparation Manager" (see page 167) for every corporate issue.

The Importance of Commentaries

The ability to **attach comments to data** is obviously important, but the actual process of developing such a system is difficult. Commentary should appear in all hierarchy levels, otherwise it tends to get lost in the mass of a corporate reporting system. At the very least, the data should contain commentary indicators, which allow the user to jump to or call up the corresponding data comments. Unfortunately, there is no data processing program that fully supports such functions. Even more important (and also missing in most software packages) is the ability to easily input commentaries throughout the corporate hierarchical structure.

The desire to have a **unified, corporate-wide system of naming conventions with consistent terminology** is, in many companies, a task too large for the Data Warehouse administrators. The administrators are responsible for helping the individual business units, not dictating their structures and terminologies. In creating and maintaining a Data Warehouse, particular attention should be paid to creating unified structures and vocabularies, as this can save a great deal of time, money and effort when consolidating corporate numbers. Experience has shown that the process of unifying structures and terminologies is lengthy and expensive, to the point that Data Warehouse managers are reluctant to force the issue on to the table.

The Problem of Making "Meaningful Comparisons"

It is relatively easy to supply system users with **historical data**. Historical data, however, is only useful if it can be used to make meaningful comparisons with current data. Formatting and structuring data to create meaningful comparisons can take a considerable effort, as it requires knowledge of the business model in addition to knowledge of the data itself.

Very few popular systems enable the user to **document data changes** at all levels of a model. Experience has shown that, although many companies desire such a feature, this missing function does not add significant business risks to an information system.

The ability to **integrate external data** in a physically independent Data Warehouse is becoming more and more important. Modern MIS software allows for the simultaneous accessing of multiple data sources, so that users can view all available data with a single application. If it is necessary, external data can also be processed outside the Data Warehouse.

Data Warehouses Can Be Built Redundancy-Free

The subject of **controlled redundancy** is becoming less and less important. Database servers and data networks are becoming so advanced, to the point that the "ideal case" of redundancy-free data storage is the norm rather than the exception. Intentional redundancies can still be found in data marts (see page 2).

3.1.2   Requirements for System Modeling and Data Access

The often-discussed **end user corporate-wide data indexes** should only be available to expert users like the information system developers. As soon as the data sets become large or complex, normal users lose their ability to comprehend and work with these indexes. Subject-specific information modules (see page 76) better meet the needs of end users.

User-Friendly Interface

A **standardized, user-friendly interface** is one of the most critical success factors. But is the interface part of the Data Warehouse or part of the information system? This question is an organizational question, and is not an important consideration in the initial development of a Business Information Shop (see page 40).

The **integration of powerful analysis tools**, which falls under the responsibility of the Data Warehouse, is not considered to be a priority in many systems. Despite the fact that these tools open up a whole new realm of data analysis possibilities, the current trend seems to be a focus on building a "normal" Data Warehouse.

The frequently mentioned desire for **flexible modeling capabilities** has not been truly solved by most software providers. Most of the popular products on the market today only fulfill a small portion of the requirements for building and maintaining a successful Data Warehouse.

Traffic Light Displays
Should be Used
Sparingly

The demand for **additional features (automatic exception reporting, warning functions, ...)** is geared more towards MIS tools. The actual value added by these features is open to debate. The claims and rosy pictures painted by marketing brochures and demo presentations often prove to be less attractive when they are applied in real business situations.

3.1.3

The Central Role of
Relational Databases

Technical Demands

Data processing managers must pay particular attention to **seamlessly integrating different computers and databases** into the existing corporate data processing infrastructure. Those responsible for the data processing systems are often quick to accept products from vendors like IBM, SAP or Microsoft; products from smaller firms, however, are often met with less enthusiasm (and sometimes outright resistance). It is very difficult for such products to gain corporate-wide acceptance. This is not the only reason that relational databases (which generally function according to common operating standards) are still largely preferred to new multidimensional data storage programs: The more robust relational databases have proven themselves to be very effective at handling large data sets ("mass data").

The need to **reduce the complexity of system management** can not be overemphasized. Otherwise, the Data Warehouse will remain the exclusive domain of the data processing department; the problem here is that data processing personnel do not feel personally responsible for managing the actual data content of the Data Warehouse. In the long run, the specific business units responsible for providing the data should be responsible for maintaining the Data Warehouse. The only way to achieve this goal is to reduce the complexity of the system management and maintenance.

"Attaching" Data
Warehouse Queries
to Operative Systems

It is important that the Data Warehouse **have no negative effects on the operative systems' performance**. The best way to prevent performance deterioration is to send queries via an "attached" module. An optimized information system can effectively access system data with acceptable query times. It is equally as important to ensure that the operative systems don't unnecessarily detract from the performance of the Data Warehouse. Running a batch procedure program on the operative system can cause Data Warehouse query times to jump from a few seconds to several minutes.

The process of making **raw data more accessible for flexible analyses** is easier to manage when relational databases are used to physically store the data. SAP®-EIS can also access relationally-stored data, using interfaces like Microsoft's ODBC.

3.2   Supplying Information

3.2.1   Data Acquisition

The ability to understand the concept of using corporate operative data as a source of raw data is essential to building an effective Data Warehouse. With this understanding, the need to physically separate operative data and Data Warehouse data is obvious. No companies today attempt to create management information systems that directly access base system data. Two considerable advantages of building a separate Data Warehouse are the ability to define standard end user reports, and the ability to easily access and make comparisons with historical data.

An "Open" Data Warehouse - A Utopian Dream?

Bigger conceptual problems arise when the actual development of the Data Warehouse begins. The "open" Data Warehouse, where all users can generate queries and develop individual analysis applications, appears to be a utopian dream. Even when good meta data is ideally structured in a Data Warehouse, the number of users who can knowledgeably work with the Data Warehouse is small and usually limited to committed analysts.

The following picture shows a typical situation for a large corporation:

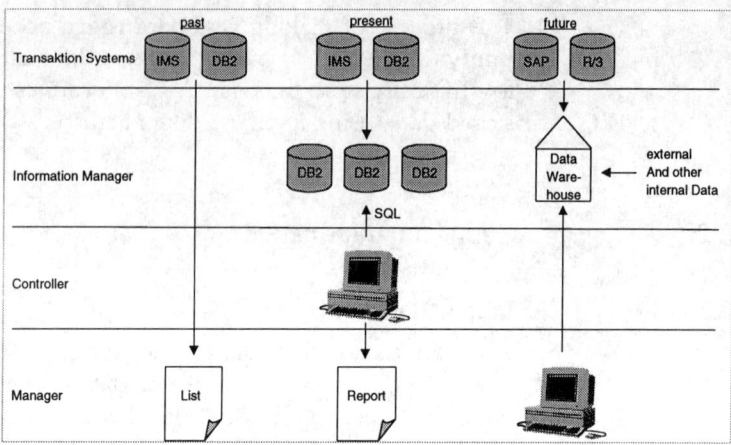

Exhibit 12: Different Interfaces to Central Data

How have managers received critical business information over the years? In the beginning, logistics systems (usually developed with COBOL and data in IMS databases) were developed, but the manager didn't have direct access to the data itself. The tried and true computer list, originally designed for use by analysts and lower-level personnel, was used by managers as a "connection" to the systems. This rigid reporting system proved inadequate for the more complex data needs of modern managers.

Separating Operative and Report Data

The practice of copying operative data into relational databases like IBM's DB2 was a revolutionary development. Using SQL, managers' finally had a tool for processing specific data requests.

It quickly became apparent how much database experience one needs to work effectively with SQL. For this reason, the use of SQL with relational databases was limited to specialists. Eventually, these specialists became responsible for creating standardized reports based on the data in the relational databases. The "EDP-supported controller" was born.

Problems Related to Data Warehouses are underestimated

Many now believe it is possible to solve all information reporting needs through a Data Warehouse. At this point in time, such beliefs have proven to be nothing more than wishful thinking. There are still a number of problems and issues related to Data Warehouses that need to be solved.

3.2.2 Information Quality Control

3.2.2.1 Responsibility

In the eyes of the end user, the information system vendor is responsible for the system contents, even though system data is usually supplied and processed by another department. One could compare the situation to a newspaper that is held responsible for the content of all the stories it runs, even though it is impossible for the newspaper to individually confirm the facts in each and every story. Although the majority of articles are taken from press agencies, the newspaper can not exonerate itself from incorrect information by blaming the information sources. From the reader's point of view, the newspaper is responsible for verifying the validity of the articles it publishes.

MIS Editorial Tasks

The same accuracy standards are applied to an MIS. A noticeable difference between the two is the fact that newspapers usually employ a number of editors, while an MIS is usually run by a skeleton crew (at least according to the marketing departments of Data Warehouse vendors).

In any case, the only way to insure adequate data quality control is to provide the information supplier and information system administrator with a reasonable supply of personnel.

3.2.2.2 Completeness

System technical processes oversee the correct and complete transmission of data. Luckily, errors rarely occur in these processes. By comparison, it is not nearly as easy to guarantee that the data being transmitted is complete with regards to the database contents. The first step in controlling data completeness is to establish clear standards and rules for evaluating data. Because there is no reliable software program that can perform data completeness checks, companies must then translate these rules into usable computer code. Processes that check for existing and known numeric entries, like number of customers or products, can be used to make determinations related to data completeness.

Data Suppliers Make Few Errors

When confronted with incomplete data, the initial impulse is to blame the information system administrator. Experience has shown that this is generally not the case. Even updates to indexes and keys occur punctually. Data suppliers are in the rule very reliable, and take their responsibilities very seriously. If a case arises where data is actually missing, perhaps because a small subsidiary was unable to meet an information deadline, data suppliers are quick to act. Ideally, the data supplier would help find the cause of the missed deadline, and help with suggestions for solving the problem(s).

3.2.2.3   Structure

Data suppliers tend to be less forthcoming with information about changes to the structure of their data. Notice of change is rarely passed along to Data Warehouse administrators. The problem could stem from the fact that data suppliers are hard-pressed to determine which structural changes will effect the Data Warehouse, and which changes won't. The data suppliers' dedication and sense of responsibility seem to end once their information reaches the Data Warehouse "black box". The issue here is a lack of communication from both sides.

Lack of
Communication

As an example, the administrators of a "pre-system" begin testing a new corporate structure for reporting forms using data sets with zeros (instead of "empty") six months before the system is to be introduced. Most of the systems and analysis tools that use the data from the "pre-system" are unaffected by this change. The information system fed by the "pre-system," however, is not equipped to deal with data in this form, and begins to supply erratic and incorrect information to end users.

The quest for software tools that can recognize and identify structural changes has been disappointing. Until such tools emerge, information system managers are best off testing random data samples and having periodic discussions with data suppliers to control for structural changes to raw data.

3.2.2.4   Deadlines

Most data is transmitted at regular time intervals according to a defined schedule. Technically this is easy to monitor (an application can be designed with a green or red "traffic light" to indicate whether the data transfer took place or not). It is a good idea to record the times that data transfers took place, so that delays or problems can be identified.

After the data supplier has time to get used to the data delivery deadlines needed by a system, real business examples have demonstrated that the suppliers become very conscientious and involved in meeting these deadlines.

Current Data Needs to be Available Quickly

It is not unusual for time lapses (sometimes several minutes) to occur between the delivery of data files and their arrival in the Data Warehouse. This can be traced to some gateway functions and copy programs, like IBM's Data Propagator, which transmit data at regular time intervals instead of being event-triggered. For some information, like current stock prices, a time lag of only 15 minutes is already unacceptable. In such cases, data suppliers and Data Warehouse administrators need to work together to find the most timely and efficient data transfer technique.

Bigger problems can also arise: One information system had problems simultaneously preparing information for both a central computer and a special server whose access was restricted to members of the board of directors. Sometimes the board members didn't receive the corporate figures until the following day, because the large amounts of data needed for the information system could only be transferred at night (when nobody was using the system). Despite the obvious advantages offered by a dedicated, user-restricted server, this data availability problem led to the removal of the board of directors server. Today, all the board members (and all other corporate users) access data directly from the central computer. That is the only surefire way to insure that information is available simultaneously for users throughout the corporation.

3.3 Inspecting Information

3.3.1 Information Assessment

Data Usefulness

The purpose of information assessment is not to identify errors. It is safe to assume that a well-designed system will produce few if any real mistakes. Information assessment should identify logical information breaks that could lead to incorrect analysis by the information user. An example should make this clearer: The production of an important raw material component occurs in a foreign subsidiary. The tax authorities in that country demand that the subsidiary show a profit. The components are then "sold" to the domestic parent company at a price that includes the subsidiary profit. The components are further processed until they are ready for sale, at which point they are sold to customers. The cost controller in the parent company uses the price including the subsidiary profit when the raw material costs of the component are entered into the domestic accounting system. The customer-driven profit results for the parent company will of course suffer under this scenario. If a manager has unlimited access to data related to this component, he will reach the conclusion that the (in reality) high profit product is a money loser. In the worst case scenario, that manager might even pull the product from the market.

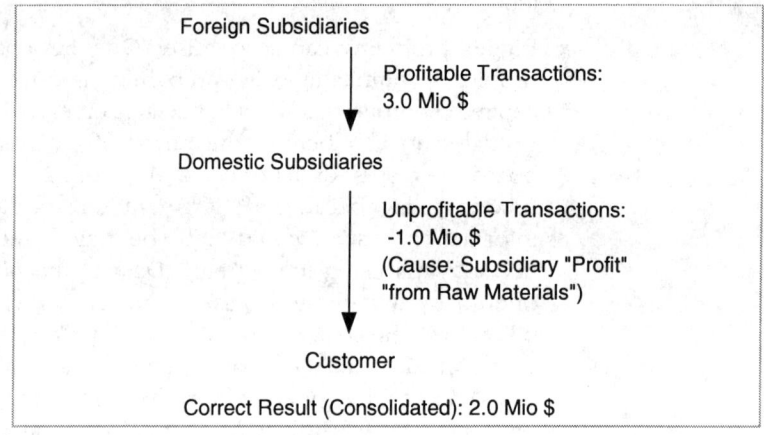

Exhibit 13: Problems with Calculating Profits

An information system administrator will experience many similar examples. A correct analysis in the example above would have used a continuous consolidation. This is of course easier said than done. But there is no doubt that an information system is better suited to call attention to important data relationships than is a traditional reporting system. A traditional system, if it was able to identify the false logic at all, would likely manually change the data or simply mention the problem in a footnote, instead of changing the analysis to reflect the real profit.

Data Usefulness

Evaluating data extracts from operative systems can provide a few shocks to the people responsible for running these "information pre-systems." These employees are always a little bit skeptical of the usefulness of this data for later analyses, but are unable to trace the source of data anomalies. This is rarely a serious problem, because the assistants and analysts in the affected business units normally know enough about the specific problem to correct or account for it. When paper reports are to be generated, they can correct or comment on unusual or implausible data entries.

In defense of these "pre-systems," it should be said that they were built to serve a completely different purpose. Today, demands are made which go above and beyond the scope of the original goals for these systems, and for which they were not designed to accomplish. Modern expectations for these systems are too high, which results in these systems getting a bad reputation within the corporation. Naturally, the system administrator's reputation suffers as well.

Until recently, many top managers were unwilling to accept this reality. They assumed that the accumulated data resources provided reliable information on a regular basis, and ignored the work of analysts and assistants who spent large amounts of time amending and correcting "pre-system" data.

Practical Example The following examples of problems in information systems highlight the explosive nature of this subject. The points in **bold** print identify particularly troublesome issues.

- Rules of Consolidation:
  - Cost Types:
    - Net results don't include commissions
    - Indent results only include results liable to commissions
    - Net and gross results for individual companies only
    - **Sales and charges between subsidiaries are not consolidated**
  - Headquarters/Domicile:
    - "Actual" and "Previous Year" results are corporate results
    - **Budget figures are corporate figures**
    - Historical data for corporation only
- Register Categories:
  - Sectors, Business Units (BU), Fields of Business (FoB):
    - Accounting delimitations based on fictitious BUs
    - Smaller subsidiaries do not always report for all BUs
    - Some BUs have unofficial FoBs
    - **some BUs report sums of several FoBs instead of individual FoB data**
  - Regions, Companies:

- – Regional BU definitions are not always official
- – A BU uses a different FoB or unit definition
- – A BU and a company are only partially owned, therefore partially consolidated on the balance sheet
- Contents:
  - Previous year data:
    - – No data corrections when consolidating "B" companies into "A" companies
    - – No "add-ons" to structural changes (BU/FoB, mergers, purchases, sales)
  - Current data:
    - – Monthly results are estimated, Quarterly discrepancies are corrected in last month of quarter, or are sometimes booked as a "correction" entry
    - – No correction of result differences in the quarterly displays
  - Budget and expectation:
    - – Missing monthly budget figures are proportionally calculated from quarterly budget figures

3.3.2   Amendments, Corrections

3.3.2.1   Information Stairway

The process by which data is gathered for a planning system can best be described as a sort of "information stairway." The source of all (actual) data are the logistic systems of the individual subsidiaries (legal entities). These systems calculate monthly results, and send data extracts to the data processing department. The data processing department is responsible for gathering and consolidating the data provided by all the corporate subsidiaries.

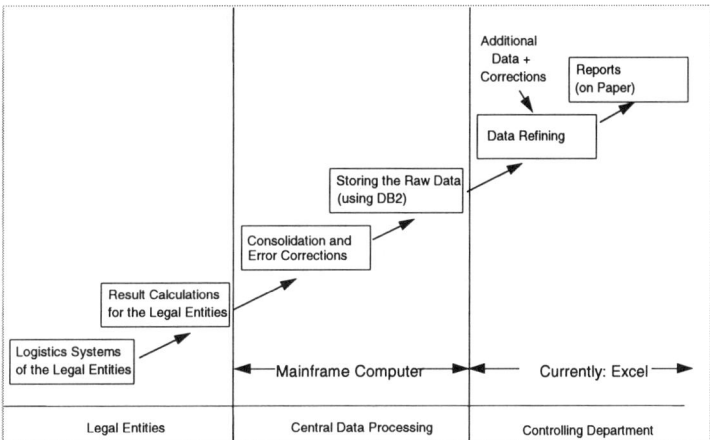

Exhibit 14: Information Stairway

Variable
Responsibility

The results are then stored on a central computer in the form of relational tables ("raw data storage"). All employees with the necessary passwords are able to access this data. Individual data records are corrected or amended ("refined") as necessary, usually de-centrally by corporate controllers or by the individual departments responsible for the data. As a safety precaution, changed data records normally can not be sent directly back to the central system. Thus, the company has no standardized file with all the corrected data records. This results in divergent data resources, some centralized and some decentralized, from which the corporate results must be calculated.

3.3.2.2   Data Processing Tools

Data Refining

As one would expect, corporate controllers use data processing tools that they are familiar with when they need to make data corrections ("data refining"). Those tools tend to be PC tools, not mainframe database tools. The consequences of this disparity can be fatal: Analyst reports (usually spreadsheet-based) often have different contents than the central corporate data tables.

On the other side, the employees in the data processing department are generally unfamiliar with PC spreadsheet programs. Because there is no common system, relations between the two departments generally run through formal channels, like contracts that specify the duties and obligations of both parties. The result is an unwieldy and time-consuming problem resolution process.

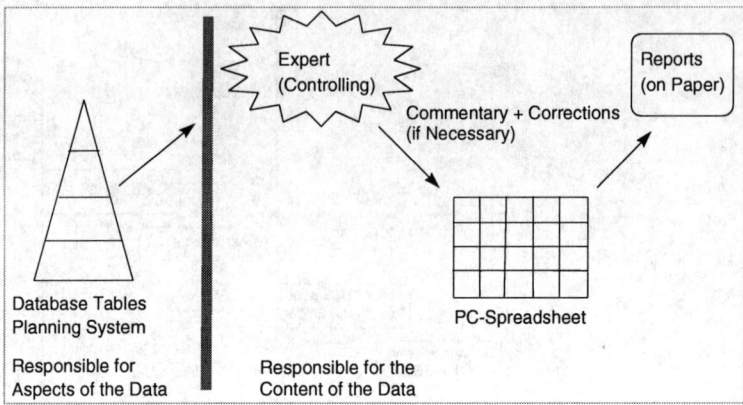

Exhibit 15: Disjointed Business Reporting Process

Multidimensional Databases

In many instances, companies are unable to pull themselves out of this data quagmire. One possible solution could be to provide controllers with easy-to-use data processing tools that contain characteristics of both database and spreadsheet programs. The most logical choice is a multidimensional database, which can be used to perform powerful and complex mathematical calculations. The problem today is that the data processing sector lacks a direct connection to multidimensional technology. Recent activities of relational database vendors with regards to multidimensional databases shows that there is hope for the future (best examples: Relational database vendor Oracle's purchase of the multidimensional tool company IRI-Express, and the purchase of MetaCube by Informix).

3.3.2.3

Data Refining

Why does a controller or analyst need to "refine" corporate data? It is difficult to define a data refining protocol, as different businesses and different departments have different management information needs. Some common data refining strategies that are used in many industries are:

- Planning for Higher Hierarchy Levels
- Displaying Planning Alternatives
- Sensitivity Analyses
- Corrections:
  - Error Corrections, i.e.:
    - Missing Entries (Data not available at a given time)

- Incorrect Entries
- Incomplete Data Entries
- Incomplete Consolidations
- No "Comparability"
- Targeted "Interventions," like:
    - Point-in-Time Bookings for Range of Time Charges (e.g. Credit Notes)
    - Fixed Production Costs (e.g., Factory Vacations, Production Line Shut-Downs)
    - Production Facility Re-Locations
    - One-Time or Unusual Charges
- Commentaries, Footnotes
- Additional Sort Criteria (Possible Cause: Changed Responsibilities)

Time Pressure on Controlling Functions

These problems can be addressed at the data source or another lower level of the information stairway (see above), but then time becomes a critical factor. It can take up to a year to incorporate new structures into an existing system. Unfortunately, a controller rarely has a year to make these changes. And once the system has been changed, it is already time to address new problems that have arisen since the last system review. Traditional data processing (using a mainframe) is a reactive rather than a proactive process.

3.3.3   Editorial Revisions

Virtual Newspaper

Thinking in terms of a virtual newspaper, "headlines" can be used to alert end users to developments or trends in their business environment. For example, notice of new monthly results or changing regulatory statutes can be provided to users, and they then have the ability to only access those "articles" that are of interest to them. By clicking on a headline, the user is immediately provided with a detailed report related to the headline theme. The newspaper format is a familiar format with which users can easily identify, and it also insures that users are aware of the most current entries available.

It would also make sense to offer users a reporting system with extensive commentary features. Editorial responsibility would fall to the individual departments. Comments are as much a part of a Data Warehouses as numeric data. The problem many companies run into is that today's database technology is not able to efficiently handle both data forms. The best solution appears to be supplementing database applications with Internet technologies, most notably HTML.

3.4   Business Information Shop

3.4.1   Architecture

inSight®: Linking Different Data Sources

Many companies store their corporate data in relational databases. The PC program inSight® provides direct access to such data via the ODBC interface. Additionally, it can also access SAP®-EIS reports (see page 61). It is further possible to display HTML format documents (i.e. from the Internet or an Intranet) within an inSight®-application. To simplify this process, the URLs (the addresses where the HTML documents are stored) can be stored in a relational database (see page 101).

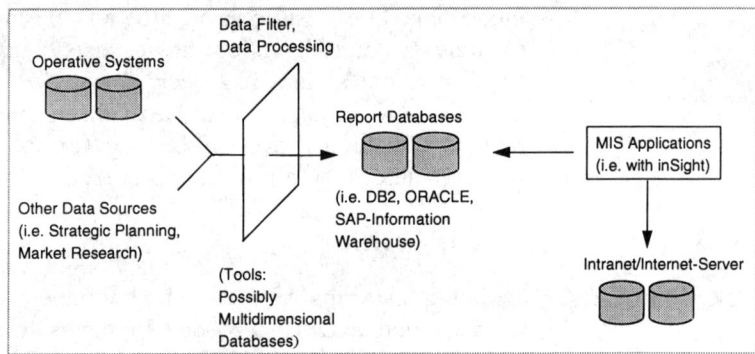

Exhibit 16: Business Information Architecture

Data Filter

In a typical system, data from the data sources (the operative systems and external data sources) is run through a data filter, where a variety of processing functions are carried out. Until recently, data filters were geared towards processing data according to hard and fast rules. Recently, however, demand has grown for a filter that is able to flexibly adapt to the needs of different users in different areas and their different task requirements. The tool that appears best suited for this challenge today is the multidimensional database.

3.4.2   Organization

Can the term "Data Warehouse" completely describe the tasks associated with supplying corporate information? Information system users shouldn't (and shouldn't be able to) simply "pick up" data from a Data Warehouse. Staying with this comparison, there is no "self service," but rather users access an application to place "orders." Access to the data is only possible through pre-defined channels. The user never has direct contact with the Data Warehouse tables, and may not even be aware that the Data Warehouse even exists.

Business Information Shop

A better term to use here is "Business Information Shop". The application is the shopping list that causes the necessary data to be retrieved "from the warehouse".

Using this terminology, the Data Warehouse is part of a Business Information Shop.

A Business Information Shop is based on the following principles:

- The Business Information Shop should not necessarily be regarded as a single organizational unit within a company. The individual functions can be distributed in various corporate divisions and departments. These divisions and departments should also be responsible for maintaining the data in their specific area of the Business Information Shop.
- Numeric data and short text entries are stored in relational databases, longer and structured text entries are stored in the HTML format (the popular Internet/Intranet language).
- MIS applications only access data from separate report tables. Data from operative systems should never be directly accessed.
- Information queries should be generated exclusively by the MIS applications, i.e. there should be no direct user-defined SQL queries to the data tables. Query tools are not allowed.
- The "owner" of the data tables has sole authority over the Business Information Shop. This makes it easier to administer access rights.
- The MIS applications within the Business Information Shop are optimized based on performance. In some cases, this will require the building of additional tables (= targeted redundancy).

Information as "Merchandise"

- To this point, users have never had to "pay" for information access. From a technical perspective, preparation should be made to develop a system for charging users based on the information they access.

A Business Information Shop consists of all the components needed to make the system work, from the gathering of raw data through the delivery of the end user modules. Usually, the raw data consists of routine extracts from operative systems. The end user modules are created using inSight®.

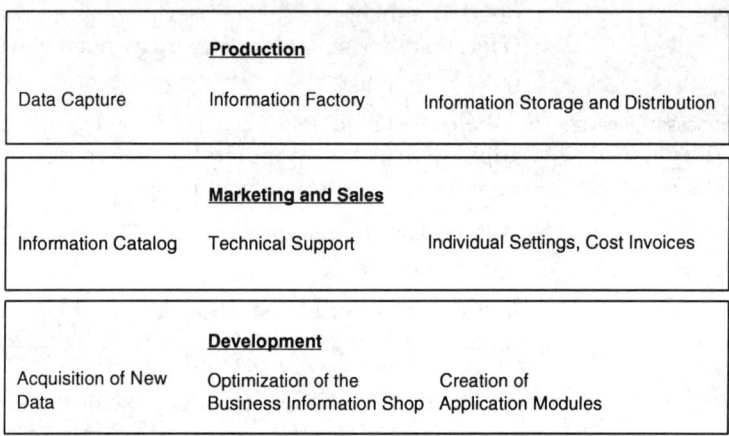

Exhibit 17: Components of a Business Information Shop

3.4.3   Business Information Shop: Production

3.4.3.1   Acquiring and Controlling Raw Data

Deadline Calendars

This area is concerned with insuring that raw system data is provided in a timely, complete, and structured form. The goal should be a completely automated data transfer process. Companies need to develop deadline calendars, where deadlines are listed for individual departments and their specific data delivery requirements. The departments should be required to enter the date and time data was delivered. Companies are thus able to develop automatic "due date/delivered date" comparisons, with a signaling or alarm mechanism that identifies missed deadlines. Routine data checks should also be programmed into the system, to insure that the delivered data is complete.

Unfortunately, notice of changes to base data is not always passed along to all system users (see also page 32). Modifications can be of several different natures, like changing column names, adding new columns, setting "placeholders" for planned-but-still-incomplete business units, new reporting categories, etc. An optimal system would include a program-supported change notification requirement from all the business units and departments supplying data to the system. Until this concept can be realized, the goal should be to develop a program with built-in data plausibility checks.

Manual Entries

Some information is manually entered or changed by the business unit supplying it. This process is used primarily for news and commentaries, but also for information regarding specific markets and countries. The Business Information Shop provides easy-to-use data input tools to facilitate manual data entry.

3.4.3.2 Processing Raw Data

Further plausibility controls need to be built into the data processing programs designed to convert raw data into finished information. Plausibility control functions need to be designed in such a way that they identify and label data outlines, so that these entries can be manually checked for accuracy.

"Comparable" Data

In today's corporate world, analysts control and correct values that are correct in accounting terms, but that often compare data that reflect completely different business scenarios. The best example is a company that acquires another company during the course of a year, and then directly compares the year-end results with the previous year-end results. A good strategy is to maintain (in addition to the original data) a second data set with "comparable" corporate structures, which the MIS application can access. One of the biggest challenges to building a successful Business Information Shop is the complex nature of designing the second data set. If this is not done correctly, it is difficult for the electronic report to compete with a paper report, where the necessary data adjustments can be made manually. To date, programs designed to amend corporate structures for reporting purposes all restructure data according to hard and fast guidelines. Powerful software tools, which are easy to use and are capable of making ad hoc changes, are few and far between (see also page 37).

Targeted Redundancy

Table structures are not always designed to provide optimal performance for MIS applications. To solve this dilemma, many companies design new tables (using extracts from existing tables) for exclusive use by MIS applications. In addition to adopting this "targeted redundancy" strategy, it is also beneficial for a company to store sum, variation, regression, consolidation, etc. calculations in these tables, to improve overall system performance (i.e. the calculations do not need to be made on the central mainframe or the client PC).

Lack of Tools for Releasing Information

When the data has been completely processed for and by the system, it needs to be examined and controlled according to a strict "data releasing" procedure. At this point in time, the tools available for data releasing are primitive at best.

3.4.3.3 Information Preparation and Distribution

Data can be stored centrally, but it can also be processed and stored locally (either the complete data set or data extracts). These scenarios include the possibility of storing data extracts on portable PCs (notebooks).

3.4.4 Business Information Shop: Sales and Marketing

3.4.4.1 Information Catalog

Business Contexts

A system's information contents should be listed in an information catalog, ordered by subject. The catalog should be available in electronic form. It makes sense to have two separate catalogs; one for managers, the other for controller/analysts. The latter group requires more detailed information, and information that identifies the source of the data. The manager catalog should focus more on broader business contexts. It is recommended that a definitive index also be provided, focusing on the system's key business context terms.

Handbook and Online Help

A handbook and/or online help feature is also a standard feature of a Business Information Shop.

3.4.4.2 Technical Support

The Business Information Shop is also responsible for insuring that the end user does not experience technical difficulties when using the information system. The installation and distribution of application and communication programs are a part of the responsibility, along with the distribution of application modules. To successfully fulfill these requirements, there needs to be a strict administrative policy with regards to version updates for both the program and the user applications. A constantly-updated MIS user registry should be a base element of any company's technical support program.

Help-Line

A help-line should also be available after the normal working day has ended. The help-line should be able to provide assistance related to content as well as technical issues. Until all the components of the Business Information Shop are completely integrated and working trouble-free, a log of all technical problems needs to be kept. This log should be reviewed periodically, and the problems identified by these reviews should be corrected as part of the system maintenance.

3.4.3.3 Individual Settings

The Business Information Shop provides customized information for individual users or user groups. Individual managers are most interested in information directly related to their area of responsibility. They expect data to be structured into meaningful relationships and logically sorted information displays. Experience has shown that, due to frequent organizational restructurings, managers' areas of responsibility are constantly changed or modified. The Business Information Shop must be capable of adapting to changing corporate structures. It therefore makes sense to centrally administer individual meta data sets, and to develop applications based on these meta data sets.

"Individualized Service"

"Individualized service" addresses the following points:

- Access rights
- Multilingual capabilities
- Local access to data
- Workflow components
- Targeted information tips
- Customized settings
- Special views, sorts, reports
- Cost invoices

3.4.5   **Business Information Shop: Development**

3.4.5.1   Acquiring New Information

One of the more time-consuming task of a Business Information Shop is the acquisition of new data. Three data acquisition scenarios are plausible:

- Act on behalf of a customer
- Negotiate on behalf of a customer
- Act on own initiative

In the first and third cases, information modules (see page 76) must be built, and files must be created. In the second case, the responsibility is transferred to another data processing area.

Creating tables, defining aliases (see page 63), and maintenance of communication files are all done according to strict rules.

3.4.5.2   Optimizing the Business Information Shop

"Road Map"

The Business Information Shop needs to be constantly scrutinized for new system improvement possibilities. This is where the concept of a "road map" can be useful. The "road map" should show the relationship between reporting goals and the database tables.

The Business Information Shop technology (i.e., the system software) should be reviewed on a regular basis as well. This holds true not only for the tools used to maintain and administer the Business Information Shop, but also for the programs and communication products used on the client side. The "standard configurations" need to be optimized so that they can be easily installed, and can then run completely error-free.

3.4.5.3   Creating User Modules

Styleguide

All the considerations discussed to this point are very important, but it is also important to develop user modules that are appropriate and informative for the ultimate end users. To create a uniform corporate appearance, to simplify overall application maintenance, and to facilitate application programming, Styleguides should be used (see page 118).

Modules and module updates should not be released to users until they have been extensively tested for reliability, and until all the involved developers agree that the application goals are met by the modules. Solutions to data processing or display problems should be as transparent and simple as possible: Complex and "acrobatic" programming tricks should be avoided. Accompanying reference documents are essential.

3.5   SAP Open Information Warehouse

3.5.1   Concept

SAP's Open
Information
Warehouse

The Open Information Warehouse (OIW) combines SAP®-EIS with other SAP information systems, like the logistics information system, the finance information system, and the personnel information system. Within the OIW, it is possible to access operative data stored outside the EIS module (ex. Logistics, Finance, Personnel), to get more detailed information. The OIW is an integrated application concept in the sense that it combines operative and strategic information systems. As a result, critical corporate success factors and other vital information are available to the right people at the right time and place.

Monitoring Critical
Success Factors

The SAP Open Information Warehouse delivers decision support information for the purpose of monitoring critical success factors. It can be applied by a wide range of end users:

- For analysts or division specialists, detailed information related to specific subjects (Logistics, Accounting, Human Resources, or other functional areas not supported by SAP) can be stored in corresponding information databases.
- For management users, a total corporate overview (or concern overview) is available with the help of SAP®-EIS. In contrast to the functionally-oriented information systems for lower level users, the management system combines information from the individual SAP systems with external data. The result is a system that enables corporate executives to monitor critical success factors from a broader perspective.

Free Navigation

The user can navigate freely within an Open Information Warehouse. For example, it is possible to access the logistics information system (LIS) or the financial information system (FIS) directly from an EIS module.

Automated procedures are available for filling the information database:

- The data supply for information systems is fed real time from transactions in the operative systems (SAP® R/3, SAP® R/2, non-SAP) via ALE (Application Link Enabling). Immediate access to daily business information is thus possible (Push Processing).
- The management information system is filled with data from the EIS. Of course, the EIS needs to be structured so that its information can be directly used by the management information system. The critical point here is to be sure that the data automatically supplied by various corporate applications and systems can be reasonably combined and compared. Data processing, in so far as the data is to be used by SAP®-EIS, needs to be structured in accordance with the needs of the MIS. This type of data delivery is best automated in periodic copy management processes (Pull Processing).

Business Intelligence

inSight® directly accesses objects from SAP®-EIS via RCF (Remote Function Calls). Unlike other software tools, which must access the base data of the Open Information Warehouse, inSight® uses the built-in "Business Intelligence" logic of the SAP analysis tools. It is therefore possible to take advantage of SAP's calculation algorithms (aggregation, de-aggregation, currency conversion, code conversion etc.) when navigating through a multidimensional data resource.

3.5.2   Assessment

There is great hope that SAP customers will be able to successfully apply this concept to their particular business models. In contrast to other software houses peddling Data Warehouse solutions, SAP's standard software offers a truly integrative solution. It is safe to assume that SAP will emerge as a leading player in the Data Warehouse marketplace.

3.6   SAP®-EIS

SAP®-EIS Is More A Tool for Controllers

SAP has established its EIS (Executive Information System) as a valuable tool in the area of corporate controlling. SAP provides three components for corporate controlling reporting needs: PCA (Profit center accounting), EIS and, beginning with version 4.0, CA (Consolidation). It is difficult to judge whether or not this is a meaningful classification system. The controller's viewpoint is the major focus of such a system, which may result in a system that fails to present information from other important corporate perspectives. This last point is a real danger, because most controlling departments are competing with other departments like accounting, finance, etc. for scarce corporate resources. As a result, controlling-driven projects often exclude data represen- tations that could provide valuable insights to these other depart- ments.

One does not get the impression from SAP, based on its marketing and press releases, that EIS is a strategic focus of the company. As a result, its information system interface (SAP-GUI) has not yet achieved a substantial market penetration relative to its customer base. It seems that SAP has recognized this fact, and in response has chosen to support the third party product inSight® (see also pages 52 and 60) as an alternative data presentation tool. A cooperatively-designed interface allows inSight® direct online access to the SAP® R/3 system. As a result, inSight® is able to access the elements in individual SAP reports. The inSight® interface to SAP® R/3 occurs over RCF (Remote Function Calls).

Integration Possibilities

SAP®-EIS can create individual corporate data pools, which collect data from the different corporate areas and their macro economic environments. SAP considers its ability to integrate the various SAP information systems (Finance Information System, Personnel Information System, Logistics Information System, Cost Accounting etc.), with each other, as well as with external data.

SAP®-EIS emulates the often heterogeneously-structured data results within closed business system data areas (Aspects). Aspects can be used to generate reports, which can be used to analyze the system data. This means that SAP can be used for "ad hoc evaluations," but also for generating structured reports. Using a "view" technology, the contents of different aspects can also be displayed in a user report.

inSight® as a Front End for SAP®-EIS

This book will not delve any deeper into the intricacies of the SAP-GUI, because inSight® is a better solution for the information concept discussed throughout the book. The contents of the solutions offered by both products are identical, because they both access data from the same data source. The real strength of this information concept lies in relying on SAP®-EIS for the information supply, and on inSight® for presenting information to the end users.

arcplan's version of inSight® that is simultaneously able to access data from both SAP®-EIS and relational databases is especially powerful. It empowers developers and users with the ability to combine and display data from multiple data sources in any number of numeric or graphic scenarios, according to the particular business need.

3.7 SAP's Business Information Warehouse

Data Warehouse is a term that is now widely used by corporations throughout the world. Many companies realize too late, however, that the expenditures budgeted for data warehouse projects have exceeded the tangible benefits of the system. The general Data Warehouse concept is based on copying data (in a technically clean manner, where the data is supplemented or modified as is necessary) from the operative systems into a separate data storage medium. Users (usually controllers) are then able to access and analyze this data with various software tools.

A corporate-wide Data Warehouse based on this concept does not offer much upside potential for a modern international corporation. While these processes seem reasonable enough from a technical IT perspective, the usefulness of the resulting data and displays have limited value in terms of explaining or mirroring actual business relationships. Controllers have developed a number of creative data processing solutions in an attempt to overcome this problem. Usually, data is loaded into a spreadsheet program on the local PC, and is then (sometimes with some additional manipulations) printed in a paper report form for distribution. The energy and time this process requires is considerable, as is the potential to improve the total reporting process.

The SAP-EIS executive information system, together with the Profit Center Accounting, Consolidation and

Corporate Planning (available in the near future) components, make up the EC - Enterprise Controlling area of the R/3 product. These modules provide highly aggregated levels of corporate data that can be used in a number of different multidimensional analyses. It should be noted, however, that SAP-EIS is not an off-the-shelf software tool for building and maintaining a corporate-wide Data Warehouse infrastructure.

These concepts and realities led to SAP's development of the Business Information

Warehouse. The Business Information Warehouse was designed with the specific needs of large corporations. This component is marketed as a stand-alone product, one that offers a standard corporate-wide solution for retrieving and processing data (with an "information-creating" component) from the various SAP systems. This is a new technology, one that justifies the use of the terms "business" and "information" in the name of the product.

SAP itself positions its new product as follows: The SAP Business Information Warehouse

- is an information pool with consolidated information from internal and external data sources,
- contains pre-configured information models and reports as well as automatic data acquisition processes,
- uses a single, standardized business process model (meta data) for R/3 applications and Data Warehouse,
- enables users to create their own unique analysis tools with the Business Explorer,
- can be quickly and easily introduced as a ready-to-go warehouse,
- provides a fast return on investment through its minimal implementation requirements, low operating costs and rapidly-realized tangible benefits,
- is an open system that can be integrated with applications and tools from other software developers.

The SAP Business Information Warehouse, currently available in release 1.2, is compatible with the new ODBC for OLAP interface; inSight is also capable of using this interface.

4

inSight® for SAP®-EIS from arcplan

4.1   Introduction

Many Proprietary
Front Ends

Many producers of data storage software for information systems, and particularly those offering multidimensional variations, also sell their own application programs (front ends). Very often, their front end is only compatible with their base product. In effect, companies lock themselves into a single software house when they select a proprietary information system solution. SAP®-EIS's graphical user interface (GUI), which only runs under SAP® R/3, is a good example. For the user, there are two significant problems that need to be addressed. First, the quality of proprietary end user tools is not always equivalent to the quality of the base software. It often seems that the user interfaces were designed for controllers and analysts rather than managers. The resulting applications tend to be missing the user-friendly qualities that are necessary to insure the success of the system. The second problem relates to larger companies running a number of different data processing systems. If a company is using several proprietary front ends that only work with corresponding database programs, managers need to learn to operate multiple systems. With the time constraints facing managers today, getting them to learn and use a single system is a challenging task. Getting them to learn multiple systems is a waste of precious resources, and very difficult (if not impossible).

Even MS Excel® is not a satisfactory solution to this problem. Most controllers are familiar with the program, and are able to quickly develop end user applications consisting of standard data display screens. The problem is, it is impossible to use the product to create a viable information system if the end users lack expert or even basic MS Excel® skills.

Unfortunately, the popular SQL query tools (at least those that are compatible with multiple relational databases) are designed more for controllers than for managers. Products designed to act as a virtual "information level" between the database tables and the end user application (meaning that they translate the complicated relational database structures into business-oriented terms and structures), have the same problem.

New Approach

inSight®, from the Düsseldorf, Germany-based company arcplan, uses a different approach. The company specializes in end user interfaces, and their product is designed to be used by managers. There is still a need, however, for application developers to create turn-key applications for the end users. The highly-flexible nature of the Windows and APPLE Macintosh compatible program makes it possible to develop applications covering a wide range of corporate reporting needs, and to leave the end users with a comfortable user interface. At the same time, the users don't have the feeling that they are restricted or "penned in" to any specific data perspective. To the contrary, practical experience has shown that inSight® offers more display variation possibilities than the typical firm will ever need.

Developing applications with inSight® is easy, and more importantly, modifying applications is equally as easy. A information system designed for usage by management can only survive if it is able to adapt to the changing information needs of the users. To be effective, a software tool must meet these requirements.

As a "front end specialist," inSight® is equipped with a very small internal database. The preferred system configuration uses interfaces to larger systems containing large sets of data records. In addition to two direct database connections, and a general ODBC interface that can be used to access relational databases, inSight® can also directly access data stored in SAP®-EIS reports.

Object-Orientation

inSight® uses object-oriented development. Available object types include traditional cell, column, row, table, radio box, and menu objects, but also text, picture, and graph objects. Special objects for OLE and HTML browsers are included in the program as well. Objects are positioned within a document, and the document is saved as a file. Because any inSight® document can be called up from any other inSight® document (assuming the user has permission to view the specific document), it is possible to develop complex applications encompassing all the contents in accessible corporate databases.

Objects can also be stored in libraries; A library saves all or part of the object properties related to display, contents, and document placement. Layout documents, which are used to centrally store combinations of objects, can be stored in a similar manner. (see also page 176).

No "Programmer" Language

No "programmer" language (in the traditional sense of the term) is used. Instead, developers work with a number of different functions, which can be coupled with a number of different event triggers. Event triggers include clicking on a button, switching the selection in a menu object, and entering new data into the system. Developers can also use "timed" functions, which execute specified tasks at developer-defined time intervals. Even the individual cells in a table object can be directly or indirectly incorporated into functions and triggers. The application construction process is correspondingly quick and easy. The ability to make objects invisible has proven to be a very useful feature. Developers can use a single document for multiple display purposes, using direct and indirect triggers to determine which objects become visible and invisible.

Automatically-Generated Query Language

The root of the program stems from the data source interfaces it offers. A separate database window is provided for defining the nature and conditions of the connections to the data sources. The contents of the data source tables can be displayed in inSight® objects. These objects use inSight®'s built-in query generator to automatically create queries for SQL databases or for SAP®-EIS. The application developer has no direct influence on the query that is generated; as a matter of fact, a developer can create powerful applications without having any knowledge of the SQL language.

Internal Database

The internal database exists in the local computer's RAM, and can be accessed just like any other database. It can be used to optimize application performance. In many cases application performance can be improved by reducing the number of data calls to a server, and by storing the results of past queries in the local computer's temporary memory. Another option is to write the query results directly to the local computer's hard drive, so that the user can access the information without physically connecting to the server (mobile computing, see page 62).

A host of administrative and documentation features round out the tool's capabilities. It is worth singling out the three help levels associated with each inSight® document. Developers can use these levels to hide (from end users) help objects that enhance application performance, but otherwise detract from the application's overall aesthetic appearance (see example on page 178).

Room for Creativity   An important characteristic of the inSight® program is that it makes application development fun. There is plenty of room for creativity on the part of the developer, although the extensive design possibilities offered sometimes lead to elaborate and "over-designed" applications. The developer should always keep the functional purpose of the application in mind when choosing a design form.

The following description of inSight® elements is not meant as a replacement for the program handbook. It is not a complete description of the program's abilities. Rather, it is an overview drawn from years of practical experience with the program, and gives an idea of the necessity of several key program functions.

4.2   Object Types

4.2.1   Overview of Object Types

14 Object Types   When the program is started, an empty document will appear on the screen. The document is the fundamental building block for an inSight® application. Unlike MS Word® or MS Excel®, information is not entered directly into the document (with the exception of the background color and pattern). Instead, there are 14 object types offering different data display possibilities, like text labels, formulas, and database entries. Four object types are used to display structured information: cell objects, row objects, column objects, and table objects. There are also five object types used primarily to make display selections and to control application functions: Menu objects, radio buttons, check boxes, buttons, and switch objects. There are similarities between these two groupings, like the fact that all nine of these objects can be used to execute control functions. However, the last five objects described are all capable of handling complex structures like formatted texts, pictures, graphs, and OLE and HTML objects.

As is standard in most Windows programs, developers can arbitrarily size objects and select their positioning within a document. The Color palette and other standard Windows optical formatting possibilities are also available. If all the display contents are unable to fit in the selected inSight object, scroll bars automatically appear in that object. Picture and OLE objects don't offer this feature, as there is no built-in capacity to size and display these data types. Column and table objects unfortunately cut off text entries that exceed their chosen sizes.

These objects include a number of additional features, among the most important being the ability to select event triggers that render the objects invisible/visible.

4.2.2   Objects for Structured Information

Table, Row, Column, and Cell Objects

Objects for structured information include the actual display tables and columns, rows, and individual cell entries. They are ideally designed to display numeric data and short descriptive text entries. A typical combination consists of a row object with column titles, a column object with row labels, and a table with numeric data. Additional column and row objects can be added to display sums. Only the objects that are furthest right and furthest below on the display appear with scroll bars. These scroll bars control all the linked objects in the screen display. There are a few unique situations where scroll bar relationships need to be switched off, but in most cases scroll bars prove to be both helpful and user-friendly.

Corporate Identity

Unlike MS Excel®, where data is displayed in a basic, rigid worksheet, inSight® offers a number of creative data display possibilities. The program's display opportunities make it easy to develop applications that emphasize (and sometimes create) a distinct corporate identity. Predefined Styleguides can be used to insure that standard display formats are used in a various corporate applications.

Mathematical operations, like building sums, are always defined for an entire object. Column objects can be used to sum the contents of a table object's rows, and row objects can be used to sum the contents of a table object's columns (The table object displays white values on a black background). A cell object can be used to add up the sum entries in a column or row object. If a value in a table object is changed, the program automatically updates all the document formulas related to that object. This is a capability unavailable in MS Excel®.

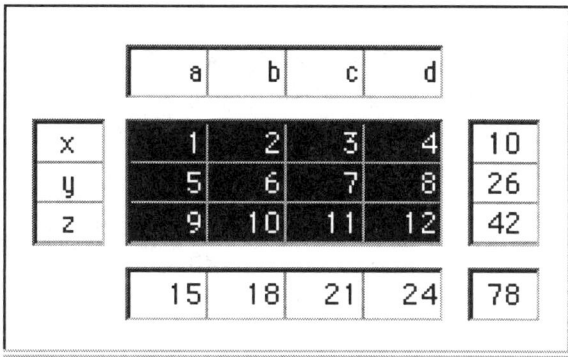

Exhibit 18: inSight® Table Objects

Individual and Collective Formats

The most interesting formatting feature is the ability to format cells individually or collectively. It is also possible to format groups of cells within an object with the same characteristics. Individual data can be collected via queries, and the cells can be color coded based on the query results. inSight®'s extensive formatting features make it possible to facilitate difficult yet reasonable formatting desires. As an example, it may be useful to individually identify changed data in an appointment planner consisting of date, time, location, and title columns. The column entry that has been changed should be colored differently from the unchanged entries. Using the "data change" information (which, like the appointment data, can be centrally stored in a database table), inSight® can easily accommodate this color coding scheme (see example page 121). The coloring is controlled by object column and row numbers, which are automatically identified when the cell is clicked on. The cells will then be color coded if the defined conditions have been met (in this case, if the information displayed in the cell has been changed).

OLAP Data Type is Planned

A multidimensional table object is unfortunately not available at this time. Such an object would make navigating in the OLAP data realm even easier. arcplan is currently in the process of developing a corresponding inSight® object type.

4.2.3 Control Objects

As has already been described, table objects can be used to control functions and navigate users through a management application. But there are also specialized objects that offer an expanded range of application features and functions.

Menus and Radio Buttons

Menus and radio buttons allow the user to select a single entry from a list of entries, like choosing England from a list of countries. The only difference between a menu and a radio button is the optical display form. In a menu, the list of entries does not appear until the user clicks on the menu object. If there is enough room in the document, developers should use radio buttons, because they enable the users to view all the available entries at all times. The selected entry is identified with a black dot (see example on page 124). Both objects have an additional feature enabling the user to select all the listed entries at once (Sum Entry), thereby creating a summarized hierarchical level across all the available entries.

Check Box

Check box objects offer a selection of yes/no conditions that can be switched on and off in any desired combination. A switch or button object triggers the desired action; with the latter method, a held-down key results in the current selection state being displayed.

4.2.4   Objects for Unstructured Information

Formatted Texts, Pictures, Graphs

Objects in this category are designed to hold or display unstructured information like formatted texts, pictures, graphs etc.., including PC files. They can be stored in a relational database, and then accessed from this database ("Pseudo BLOB"). You are not able to display PC files in inSight®. PC files can, however, be written back to the hard drive, which is an important function for updating documents.

Graph objects showcase inSight's vast performance spectrum, which is equal to that of any presentation software package available today. They completely meet the graphic display needs of modern corporations; one of the more impressive features is the three-dimensional portfolio graph.

Structured text objects, which can store font types, font sizes, font colors, and font styles (and to a limited extent tabs and returns), automatically generate scroll bars if the display selection is larger than the display object. Unfortunately, it is not possible to use these objects to reference other objects, so it is not possible to create variable text displays. This can only be done with text-filled cell objects, where the formatting is selected for the entire text passage (and not for individual characters).

OLE and HTML Objects

OLE and HTML objects display interesting connections to other PC technologies. OLE objects not only allow the user to modify data with Microsoft programs like MS Word® and MS Excel®, but they can also be stored in relational databases. inSight® can then access the objects directly, without the end user needing to have the corresponding Microsoft programs installed on the local PC. This astonishing technological achievement has a number of practical uses. For example, portfolio graphs can be created using MS Excel®, stored in the protected environment of a department server, and accessed by end users of an inSight® application.

The contents of the unstructured information objects described here can be stored centrally, as long as the relational database doesn't use special fields for these object types. Normal text cells can be used, in which inSight® stores the objects (broken down into individual character strings).

4.3   Access Methods

As an "information display specialist," inSight® is equipped with a number of powerful and easy-to-use features for filling display objects with data from central information sources. Depending on the interface used, inSight® automatically generates the appropriate data retrieval query. This saves the application developer the time and effort usually needed to create and customize application queries. A database window displays the available tables (with their table columns), which the developer can drag onto inSight® objects with the help of the PC mouse. There is no need to use any formula language like OLE or SQL. The end user is completely unaware of the various data sources accessed and the queries used to retrieve the information. The only time the user notices the underlying system data sources is when the application is started, and data source passwords need to be entered.

Query Language Generator

inSight® has proven to be a powerful "query language generator" for accessing various data storage systems. The simple data retrieval method it uses greatly reduces the occurrence of error responses related to queries, and makes it easy to modify or expand existing applications. In contrast to most SQL-based query tools, it is possible to use inSight® to generate query cascades. Thus, the results of one query can be used to formulate a second query, etc. Complex applications often send five or more "pre-queries" to a data source before the displayed data is retrieved. The purpose of these "pre-queries" is to decrease the demands on the end user, and increase the overall application comfort level. Despite these "behind the scenes" queries, the application performance level remains acceptable to end users.

Automatic Mixing of Register Texts

The macro commands used to fill objects with data can be defined in the so-called "connection mode," meaning that the formulas are created using mouse-driven connection lines between objects instead of coded texts. In the case of relational databases, register texts can be mixed together automatically, even over combination keys. It is very easy to define a menu or other display object so that it only displays those texts for which values exist in the table.

inSight® offers developers the ability to construct complicated database queries without having to directly input SQL statements. It should be noted that developers will need to spend some time familiarizing themselves with the program before they will be able to fully exploit its query generation capabilities. When a developer is comfortable with the program interface, it is easy to literally create fully functional applications in a matter of days. The actual database queries generated by inSight® can be viewed, but they can not be modified. Many users feel this is an advantage, because inSight® objects can also be used to directly input developer-defined database queries.

4.4   Interfaces

Ideally, developers generate database queries using the graphical inSight® object interface. Understandably, inSight® can not always fulfill this goal, as different data storage systems operate under different data retrieval standards. Within a given storage medium family, like relational databases, inSight® comes very close to achieving this goal. Using a conversion script, it is very easy to port an application from one relational database system to another (assuming that the table structures are the same in both databases). Unfortunately, it is not (yet) possible to include the name and location of the database system as a parameter, so it is not possible to realize an application-driven database system "switcher."

Numerous Interfaces are Supported

inSight® currently supports interfaces to SAP®-EIS Reports, to SAP's Open Information Warehouse (beginning with SAP Release 3.1 G), to relational databases, to MIS-AG's multidimensional database, to the multidimensional cubes from Informix and ORACLE, and to MIK's data cubes (MIK is a German-based software house that specializes in planning and controlling software). The interface to SAP®-EIS is especially worthy of mention, because inSight® accesses the aggregated data from SAP Reports (see also page 49). Other tools have to use the ODBC interface to retrieve base data from the underlying SAP®-EIS structures. The fast connection over SAP OLE controls is used to create the initial interface to the SAP Automation Server (3.0 B-D).

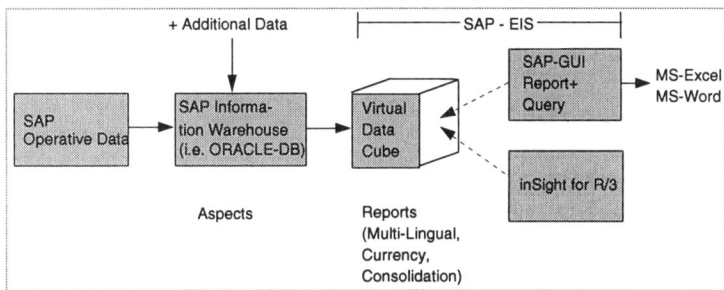

Exhibit 19: Accessing SAP®-EIS with inSight®

Beginning with SAP release 3.0 D, inSight® supports the following functions and features for accessing SAP®-EIS:

- Simultaneous access to multiple SAP®-EIS Reports
- Queries to any hierarchy levels
- Display of calculation tables
- Use of sorting features
- Top "N" Lists
- Hierarchy displays
- Use of variables

In general, linking to an SAP® R/3 report is different from linking to an SQL database. A connection to the base data occurs when the SAP report is generated, so it is not necessary to repeat this step. In some cases, it may make sense to link objects from different SAP reports. For example, it makes more sense to use a single "Customer" selection menu to access data from two different reports, than to create two separate selection menus. With inSight®, it is possible to define this type of object link.

When dealing with hierarchies, a difference must be drawn between inSight® and SAP hierarchies. SAP hierarchies are not strictly defined. Using regions and countries as an example, some regions may have countries ordered directly below them, while others will have a country grouping level in between.

inSight®'s SAP interface also supports the operators used to create the so-called "TOP N" queries. The end user can use this function to display the ten largest customers, the ten smallest customers, or all the customers responsible for 80% of total turnover.

inSight® is equipped with special functions related to the direct SAP® R/3 interface. These functions are designed to take advantage of the strengths and unique features in the SAP® R/3 program.

Positive Experiences

With regards to the ODBC interface to relational databases, countless successful systems that use this interface have been built over the past several years. One can safely refer to this as a stable technology. Popular databases for such systems include central systems like DB2 under IBM's VTAM, ORACLE, Informix and SAS, as well as decentralized local tables like DBase or MS Access®. The locally-installed SQL Server from Microsoft, has proven to be an extremely powerful solution, especially under Windows NT. Other interfaces are newer and have less practical experience, and are therefore not addressed here in great detail. The fact that they are enthusiastically greeting the chance to work with inSight® indicates the respect the program has earned in the information system industry. A key credibility factor is the relationship with SAP, as exemplified by the joint development of inSight®'s direct interface to SAP® R/3.

Local Data Storage

inSight® can store data locally, in the PC's main memory. Temporary data is stored here, and is retrieved using normal SQL commands. Many developers are using the local storage feature to improve application performance, because it enables users to "load" large data blocks and query them without needing to continuously access a central server. Since locally-stored data is written directly to the hard drive, it is possible to develop mobile applications. Such applications need to be regularly updated with current data to insure that end users are analyzing the most current information available.

Connections

inSight® creates two additional files for every connection: a connection file containing technical data, and a repository file containing descriptions of database tables and columns. The repository file regulates things like aliases (for joining columns from different tables). Another repository file feature is the ability to define how inSight® should interpret column contents (i.e., a numeric entry in the form "120568" should be interpreted as the date 12/05/68).

4.5   Functions

4.5.1   Events

No Programming Language

inSight® does not use a "programming language" in the traditional sense of the term. The calculation and control functions offered are numerous and versatile. Event triggers can be used to launch various functions defined in inSight® objects or documents. These events include:

- Calculation
- On Update
- On Input
- On Confirm
- On Mouse Click
- Output
- Cursor Inside
- Cursor Outside

Complex Function Sequences

The ability to use events to control functions opens a wide spectrum of processing and navigation possibilities. Consequently, the individual objects only offer control triggers consistent with the nature of that object type. The last two events in the list above relate to actions controlled by dragging the mouse over an object. These functions are generally used to bring about a new cursor appearance, or to display an object-specific information text in inSight®'s information line.

inSight® documents themselves recognize four additional events:

- On Open
- On Close
- After Printed Page
- On Key

An internal optimizing feature causes the individual functions to be executed in a logical procession.

4.5.2   Calculation Functions

Spreadsheet
Functions

This function group can be found in some type of similar form in every spreadsheet program. The mathematical functions operate according to the spreadsheet program standards and syntax common to the industry. Formulas are defined for an entire object, although individual cells in multi-celled objects (like table, column, and row objects) can be directly and indirectly referenced. Statistical and business-related formulas are used to functionally supplement the "normal" calculation functions.

Particular note should be taken of the excellent handling and processing of time elements and text strings. More exotic functions like arc tangent etc., whose practical use in a business application is very limited, are still included in the package.

4.5.3   Layout Functions

Layout functions are advanced event-triggered display features that identify important data values, trends or variations. These functions go well beyond the familiar "traffic light" function. As an example, users are able to highlight individual entries from a list (whose entire list of entries can be displayed with a two-color scheme for easier reading) with a different background and font color, based on an event trigger (see example page 121).

Broad Spectrum of
Graphing
Possibilities

The broad spectrum of graphing possibilities provides creative developers with an almost endless wealth of information display choices. Most of these functions can not be used with event triggers. Graph objects use specific dialog windows to define the data objects whose contents are to be displayed.

4.5.4 Control Functions

A listing and description of all inSight®'s control functions is neither possible nor meaningful in the context of this book. For those readers interested in a more in-depth look at inSight®'s full functional capabilities, the program handbook is recommended.

Very Powerful Tool

The power of these functions, as welcome as they are, make it essential that application developers devote a large chunk of their time resources to working with and understanding the nuances of the inSight® program. New features and options are constantly being added to the program, and, as is customary with most software programs, inSight® developers lack the time to fully explore the added versatility (and complexity) of the new functions. This is not meant to be a condemnation of corporate MIS developers. They are charged with the task of getting fully functional applications up and running under extreme deadline pressures. Regardless of where the pressure is coming from or who is responsible for getting the job done, the fact is that inSight® makes almost every type of corporate reporting need possible. Sometimes only experienced developers are able to find the proper solution to a reporting need, while inexperienced developers produce constructions that are confusing and fail to meet performance requirements. To create simpler (and therefore more economical) applications, developers need to be educated in the basics of application development with inSight®.

Interactive Control Opportunities

The interactive (in this case meaning "user-driven") control opportunities are extremely powerful, because they operate according to flexible parameters related to specific columns and rows in document objects. It is thus possible to create completely menu-driven user interfaces, so the end user is able to operate the application without the use of a keyboard. The VISIBLE/INVISIBLE function (see page 56) plays a key role in many development strategies, as it enables developers to create several different data displays within a single document. The result is more compact applications and a reduction in redundant development steps.

Indirect control functions include event-driven functions (for example, functions that are launched when the selection in a menu object is changed), actions that are started or repeated according to a defined time schedule, viewing only those entries that meet defined criterion, saving values and pictures in a database, and the launching of external programs. Because developers are able to build "function groups," which are bundled together and triggered by an EXECUTE command, it is possible to limit the number of functions that need to be associated with specific display objects. It is thus easier to debug and maintain applications as a whole, and end user display screens more specifically.

4.5.5 **Report Functions**

The reporting functions (for generating paper reports) in the inSight® program offer a reporting solution comparable to specialized software packages available on the market. For typical daily, weekly, or monthly reporting needs, the functions available in inSight® are more than adequate.

4.6 **PC Platform**

Compatible with APPLE Macintosh Computers

inSight® applications run on Windows and APPLE Macintosh computers. Only the connection files (see page 63) are platform specific.

In terms of Windows operating systems, the NT, Windows 9x and (with the installation of WIN32S) Windows 3.1x systems can all be used to run inSight®. With the Macintosh OS, a 68xxx version and (a much faster) Power-PC processor version are available. With the exception of a few minor differences, an application will run identically on all these operating systems. Companies with a large number of APPLE Macintosh computers can reap massive benefits from inSight®'s cross-platform compatibility. Because OS/2 lacks a Windows 9x emulation, it is not possible to run inSight® under the OS/2 operating system. There are no immediate plans for an OS/2 or a UNIX inSight® version.

Lack of Support for Older Operating Systems

The older Windows 3.1x and Macintosh operating systems using the 68xxx processors run the risk of becoming obsolete in terms of future Microsoft technological developments. The ActiveX technology (inSight® Internet Edition, see page 180) and the tools for embedding HTML objects (see page 59) are two examples of such technologies.

The inSight® program, like individual inSight® applications, can be installed on a PC or on an application server. This is true for the developer version as well as for the Runtime version (in which no changes can be made to the application). In Runtime mode, developer-defined central function buttons and a developer-defined menu tool bar can be used.

5 Building an Information System

5.1 Project Organization

5.1.1 Initiator

A critical success factor for major corporate projects is the support of a high-ranking executive. This is particularly important when trying to build a comprehensive information system, because the entire process often turns out to be more complicated and time-consuming than originally planned.

Sponsor

The concept of a project sponsor was developed along this line of thinking. Conventional thinking dictates that for a project to be taken seriously throughout the company, the sponsor should be a board member or hold an otherwise influential position. Furthermore, the sponsor's support for the project should be seen as unconditional.

Sponsors play an important role in promoting major corporate projects. But focusing solely on the sponsor concept can cause a company to ignore the need to develop the right organizational structure for an information system project.

When a single individual sponsors a project that lacks widespread support among other important executives, there is the very real danger that the project will be viewed as that individual's "pet project." If the sponsor loses interest in the project (which is not an uncommon occurrence), or moves to a new position in the company, the project loses both support and resources. In the past, this predicament has meant a quick death for many promising information system projects. This problem is an organizational issue: A successful project requires a stable project support infrastructure.

The "Sponsor" Model Is the Second-Best Solution

The "sponsor" model is a good model, but for situations requiring a large time investment (like the development of a corporate-wide information system), it is really the second-best solution. The biggest weakness is often perceived as a strength, namely that the project is always associated with that single person. If the sponsor leaves or is forced out of the company, the project is likely to die or be "redesigned" out of existence.

Board of Directors as a Customer

It is better to organize the project according to a sponsor-customer model, where an important corporate executive (the "sponsor") is responsible for monitoring and reporting project progress to the "customer" (for example, the Board of Directors). This structure protects the project against personnel changes, because project responsibility is associated with a position, not a personality. If the project has a clearly-defined customer, goal, and timeline, it will proceed regardless of the career path of the sponsor. In real business situations, the sponsor-customer model has proven itself as a robust, effective model.

5.1.2   Project Group Selection Criteria

Information and System

The name "information system" makes it clear that there are two distinct components to the term: "information" and "system." In large corporations today, there is no central group responsible for the preparation of internal information. Instead, this task is broken down into smaller assignments for various departments, who distribute the results of their analyses in paper form. The assignments tend to fall to controllers and analysts, but also to departments like finance and accounting. Their clientele are the end users who are the target group for a data processing department-supported information system. Because of this inherent conflict, an adversarial relationship between the existing information suppliers and the group responsible for the information system is virtually guaranteed (at least initially).

Download

Divisions and departments within a corporation are moving more and more towards centralized corporate data sources (mostly relational databases), whose contents come from operative systems. The data processing department is generally responsible for insuring that the system is functioning correctly. The popular tactic of "downloading" data to a local PC, and then "processing" the data with tools like MS Excel® spreadsheets, usually presents a corporation with a common problem: The centrally-stored data is changed or commented upon at the local level, but these local changes can not easily be sent back to the central storage device. The paper reports used by decision-makers are therefore sometimes very different from the original output from the central data system. In this environment, it is difficult to develop popular data processing department-supported information systems, or any system that feeds on information from a central data source.

Employees within the different divisions and departments are usually capable of creating impressive information display screens using PC spreadsheet, text, and graphic programs (see also page 37). When it comes to generating even the simplest database queries, however, they are not as confident. The reason for this can possibly be traced to the expert knowledge needed to design an efficient system of central database tables. Another explanation could be the fierceness with which many data processing departments protect their "territory" from "outsiders," and the resulting reluctance divisional employees have to get involved with the technical aspects of the system.

Database Knowledge

There is no denying that one of the strengths of the data processing department in a large corporation is their knowledge of and ability to work with a number of different database systems. This is especially true with standard transaction and analysis software packages. Currently, SAP and its SAP® R/3 System set the industry standard. In contrast to this knowledge, data processing employees are generally less familiar with spreadsheet programs like MS Excel® than divisional employees. This knowledge disparity presents an opportunity for smaller, external consulting firms, who are able to speak the same language as the divisional employees. Even a basic term like "operative" has a different meaning for divisional employees and data processing employees. Divisional employees distinguish decisions and information as being either "strategic" or "operative," while data processing employees discuss systems that are either "operative" (i.e. up and running), or "non-operative" (i.e. under development or no longer running). Definition problems like this, along with a tendency to over-use the technical jargon associated with one's functional area, make communication between these two groups difficult.

Lack of Experience

Taking all these issues into consideration, the most formidable question becomes, "What is the best design for the project group responsible for building an information system?" Who should lead the project group, and who should monitor the group's progress? For many companies, it quickly becomes apparent that there is no person within the organization with the concrete experience needed to lead the project group. Unfortunately, this realization is rarely incorporated into strategic corporate planning. The building of an information system is thought to be an easy task, and the powerful sales pitches of information system product vendors reinforce this misconception. These vendors recommend identifying an information need, then buying a system and software to solve the need. The complexities associated with actually designing and implementing a comprehensive corporate-wide information system are completely ignored.

Formidable Challenge

The truth is that building an efficient information system is one of the most formidable challenges facing modern corporations. But again, most companies fail to recognize an information system's importance. Few companies have developed evaluation criteria for information system project groups, or designed career paths for information system or Data Warehouse managers.

Critical Comments

These preceding comments are very critical; most executives would likely deny that they accurately reflect the situation within their companies. But the issues raised here are significant, and they illustrate the difficulties involved with developing a general plan for an information system design and implementation project group.

Information system project groups are often dominated by data processing experts. Group members from the functional divisions are usually assigned supporting roles, often to overly-generalized duties like defining the overall project objectives (which is often difficult if not impossible). An alternative project strategy, which likely grew out of executives' dissatisfaction with centralized, dominant data processing departments, is to employ external consultants for critical IT issues. The logical extension of this policy is increased project input for the functional departments, because the external consultants are forced to treat them as true "customers." Because of the extremely competitive consulting environment, external project members are inclined to delve into the intricacies of the problem, instead of simply attacking the problem's symptoms. They seldom demand or request system requirements and system specifications. Prototyping is usually the basis for information system developing. There are two important reasons to doubt the long-term viability of projects using external consultants. First, most consultants lack practical experience with large-scale information systems. Second, and perhaps more important, is the indisputable fact that no information system can perform effectively and reliably without the support of the data processing department. Given the complex nature of linking data processing systems, and providing these systems with meaningful raw data, it is crucial that the data processing department be integrated in any large-scale information system projects.

Project Group Leader

The ideal project group (in terms of membership and responsibility) exists only as a theoretical concept. This is also true for selecting the ideal project group leader. The leader, in addition to dealing with technology issues, must also define a strategic direction for the project, and create an internal identity for the group members. A good project leader would be an experienced internal employee from a functional department, one who is willing and able to devote both time and effort to understanding and solving data processing problems. Such a commitment is necessary, because there are no turnkey technology solutions available today.

Dearth of Experienced Employees

Most companies do not have internal employees who have experience in designing and implementing corporate-wide information systems. To add to this problem, the real decision makers within a company rarely have any idea of the complexities associated with major data processing projects. As a result, the criteria for establishing project goals and timelines are ambiguous at best, as are the criteria for evaluating project member skills and abilities. Employees are often judged to be "appropriate" project team members based on illogical standards like proficiency with PC spreadsheet programs. Little if any consideration is given to the employee's ability to conceptualize solutions for actual information system problems.

Babylonian Communication Problems

The members of project groups assigned to build an information system are generally selected using an arbitrary process of representing all the involved or affected functional departments and divisions. The various divisions and departments, like controlling, finance, individual business units and data processing each provide a project group member. Early project group meetings are often slowed down by the resulting "Babylonian" communication problems.

Casual observation confirms the notion that data processing experts, skilled though they may be with database designing and maintenance, are generally inexperienced with spreadsheet programs like MS Excel®. At the other extreme, most controllers are gifted spreadsheet users, but lack any experience with databases. This is not the only conflict likely to arise in a project group whose members have diverse corporate backgrounds. The actual information itself often contains proprietary meaning that the various departments and divisions are reluctant to share with one another. Further, the project group members see themselves as defenders of their departments/divisions, and they are reluctant to consider opinions or suggestions that fail to advance their departmental or divisional agendas. The results achieved by such a group are often compromise solutions; it is difficult (if not impossible) for the group members to objectively and independently develop solutions for the immediate and long-term problems they are charged with resolving. The leadership skills and overall business and technological abilities of the project leader greatly influence the ability of the project group to achieve its realistic goals.

Is it possible to put together a successful project group out of a collection of inexperienced employees? Can a project group be successful with a project group leader experienced in organizational matters, but who lacks information system knowledge? The answers to these questions, based on numerous real business experiences, is clear: No. To date there are very few examples of truly successful large-scale information system projects. Perhaps this is because the project groups responsible for information system projects are assembled using the above-mentioned guidelines. The same issues appear to confront the larger information system software vendors as well, as they have yet to develop standardized successful implementation processes.

Careful Project
Group Selection
Process

Therefore, it is necessary to exercise a great deal of care and tact in putting together the project group. If a company lacks qualified personnel for such a project, it makes sense to "groom" possible project members using smaller, related projects. The knowledge and expertise they develop on the smaller projects can be the difference between the success or failure of a corporate-wide information system project.

5.1.3   Project Leader Requirements

Constantly-Changing
Requirements

There is another reason why the project leader should have a good understanding of technology issues to complement an understanding of the information content itself. An unpleasant reality of information system projects is the fact that the project demands are difficult to define before the project is started. They grow as the project develops, and multiply as the system put into operation. Nor are the expectations for an MIS static (see also page 187). The end users expect new technologies to be integrated into both the underlying system and their user interfaces. As an example, portable access to the system (mobile computing) may be a non-issue during the project planning phase, but may become the central issue as the project progresses. It is not a good idea for the project leader to use earlier agreements or definitions in an attempt to limit the scope or scale of the project. The leader must be able to realistically assess the costs/benefits trade-off of various proposed additions to the project.

Project Committee

The larger project goals should be defined and monitored by a powerful person or entity within the company, preferably a project committee with a board director or senior vice president. The political influence of such a project committee member can be vital to keeping the project on track in the event of technical problems or unanticipated delays. The steering committee needs to recognize that many of the project group members will have no concrete experience in the information system area. This is true even for the project group members from the data processing department, whose strengths tend to be focused on operative systems (transaction systems). Operative systems are very different (both in their purpose and structure) from information systems. The traditional, data processing department-suggested model for designing successful transaction systems (with system requirements, system specifications and a data model) can not be simply extrapolated and applied to building an information system. The next section of this chapter will address the question of whether or not the development of an information system requires a fundamentally different plan of action.

5.1.4 Plan of Action

Every data processing department in a medium or large corporation uses a defined system for creating and introducing software and software upgrades. The basis for these systems are the system requirements, with a data model as an essential component, and the system specifications.

System
Requirements

The system requirements list the system users' functional demands and requirements for the system that is to be programmed (system definition). Components of the system requirements include the overall system concept, the entity relationship diagram, the functions tree and the information flow diagram, as well as a listing of the resources available for the data processing technical solutions. A data model can be helpful in identifying the relationships between the individual terms (entities) used in the system.

System
Specifications

The system specifications define the technical details for the system, identifying the capabilities and limitations the project group will face.

After the users and developers "agree" on the basic structure for the system, the system requirements and system specifications can be converted into programming code. Today the trend is towards the use of standard software, as opposed to earlier attempts to develop proprietary corporate software programs. Standard software programs offer advantages in that they provide ready-to-use system solutions that can be (relatively) easily modified to meet the different needs of different companies. SAP uses the term "customizing" to describe these modifications. Of course, the customizing process must be executed for every standard software package used, and may require additional resources when upgrades are installed. Those companies that continue to use in-house programming can expect to reap the benefits of so-called "RAD-Tools" (RAD = Rapid Application Development), which offer the promise of high-quality graphic user interfaces and reduced development time.

Interfaces, Base Data

It is especially important to carefully design the interfaces from the operative systems to the information system, as well as the data repositories and data registers. From a technical perspective, a successful system is one that is robust, reliable and available to all designated users.

The data processing department will no doubt agree with this system design process, because it has proven effective in countless projects. These projects are, however, very often logistics-oriented projects, where the relationships between the entities are very important. It is important to note if a customer operates from only one location, or if they operate multiple production facilities. It is also important to be able to track the entire transaction process, from the order receipt, through the credit check, through the pricing decision, and the actual production and quality control of the goods, right down through shipping and billing. Such a process chain requires a system design like the one described above.

But the process has yet to bear fruit in projects focusing on the design and construction of information systems. This is probably because information systems have a completely different structure from operative systems. They deal with dimensions whose data can include summarized data spanning multiple hierarchical levels. Relations between the entities play a less important role, because the evaluation tools used to process the data automatically recognize and display these relationships.

Another difference is the fact that an information system can perform multiple analyses on a data set. Operative systems operate according to fixed output guidelines, and are not designed to provide flexible result displays.

Information Quality

The biggest difference between operative systems and information systems is that the information (data) that is entered into an operative system must already be present in an information system. An information system can not, therefore, be better than the actual information it contains. Consequently, the whole information gathering and quality control process is extremely important in the development of an information system.

New Procedure

When building an information system, it is a good idea to identify the "agreement with the user" with the terms dimension hierarchy definition, data usefulness analysis, and data availability analysis (see page 172) in place of data model, system requirements and system specifications. After the concept has proved theoretically viable, the next step should be to start a prototype. The best way to prototype is to involve a (or some) user(s) in the system development. The users will be most interested in building a theme-oriented information module. Developing a good user interface and visualizing the information's impact on business decisions should be the prime considerations. The critical success factors are flexibility, user-friendliness (if the system is fun to use, this can be an advantage) and system performance. This new development strategy has unfortunately yet to find widespread acceptance with the data processing community, perhaps due to their lack of experience with the paradigm.

There are also considerable differences in the profiles of information system users and operative system users. The latter are usually specialists who spend most of their time working with the operative systems. Very often, they have been working with the same systems for years, so they are used to the peculiarities and idiosyncrasies that occur in the individual operative systems. Information system users, on the other hand, can not and do not want to learn the intricacies of the applications they use. Their chief concern is quick access to the data they need to make strategic decisions. If user acceptance of an information system is low, the process of gathering the necessary information is delegated to assistants (which may partially explain the explosive growth in staff positions at major corporations over the past few years).

The following summary compares the fundamental strategies used to develop operative systems and information systems:

	Operative	**Information**
Class	Relations-Driven	Dimensions-Driven
Preparation	System Requirements System Specifications Data Model	Dimension-Hierarchy Definition Data Usefulness Analysis Data Availability Analysis
Realization	a) Standard Software b) Rapid Application Development	Prototyping Modular Development (Business Objects)
Key Terms	Register, Interfaces	User Interface, Visualization
Success Factors (From a Technical Perspective)	Robustness Reliability Availability	Flexibility User-Friendliness (Fun) Performance
IT Acceptance Level	High (Classical Process)	Low (Little Experience)

Exhibit 20: Differences in Development and Expectations

5.2   Determining Information and Communication Needs

5.2.1   Fundamental Procedure

No Standardized
Rules

To put it bluntly: An exact plan for determining information and communication needs does not exist, and is not likely to exist in the near future. Different people, different divisions of responsibility, and constantly evolving corporate priorities make it difficult to establish a blueprint for a long-term information system strategy. A manager who has worked for years in the same area will concentrate on implementing changes that are subtle and (for an outside observer) unspectacular. On the other hand, a manager who recently took over a new position will act very differently. Before the second manager can make any positive contributions to the information system, he needs to become familiar with the unique demands of his position.

Topical Subjects
Have Priority

Topical subjects like turnover tracking, personnel issues, currency fluctuations, raw materials supplies, etc. tend to eclipse general responsibilities, often for weeks at a time. This offers a good explanation why the same manager will have different information needs if asked at different points in time. From the time an information system concept is formed to the time it is brought online for managerial use, interest in the system may dwindle. Even worse, some managers may insist that the focus of the system be redefined. Referring back to agreed upon documents and contracts may soothe the developer's ego, but will not have much of an impact on gaining end user acceptance for the system.

A sound (but difficult to implement) strategy is to offer management only the information they need to carry out their specific corporate functions. It is almost impossible to define what information is needed by what managers. Further, restricting managers' access to information blatantly ignores the fact that many managers need to be aware of what is happening in other divisions, and that managers should be responsible and intelligent enough to determine what information they need and when they need it. A well-intentioned system with restricted data access can end up having a negative effect on corporate decision-making. Because of these risks, true restricted data access systems are uncommon in the corporate world.

What, When, How

Thought needs to be given to the purpose and goal of the system. Managers and analysts set different priorities with regards to answering the questions "WHAT," "WHEN" and "HOW." Strategically-oriented managers are most interested in issues related to WHAT, then WHEN, and lastly HOW. A new product launch illustrates this point clearly: It is important to decide which product to bring to market (WHAT), then to decide on the timing of the product introduction (WHEN), and then to decide on HOW the launch should be executed. This prioritization plan stems from the years of experience that a top manager has, and from the tendency such managers have for making important decisions based on "gut feelings." The actual product launch is then executed by marketing employees.

The situation is completely different for an employee in the operative field. Here, the primary interest is addressing the issue of HOW. Price setting belongs in this category. The next priority is on WHEN, and then finally on WHAT. The lack of emphasis on WHAT makes sense when one considers that these issues are usually addressed directly by top managers.

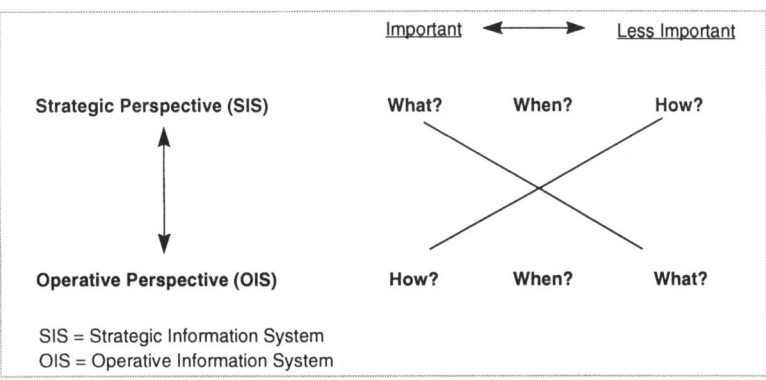

Exhibit 21: Different Perspectives

Different System Requirements, Same User Interface

Since strategic and operative users have different priorities, it makes perfect sense that their systems be built differently. That doesn't mean that different technologies should be used to build the systems. The difference should be solely in the content of the information displayed.

Recognizing the differences between strategic and operative systems doesn't address the issue of what information is needed.

An additional problem is that once information needs have been identified, the desired information is not always available. And building a new data processing department-supported system to provide that information is a risky endeavor. It's not enough to simply build a data structure. The data itself must be constantly updated, and data quality must be maintained. Achieving this goal often takes much more time than is initially expected. In some cases, the creation and maintenance of such a system is impossible.

Pragmatic Approach to Implementation

In the initial stage of an IS project, it is important to ascertain the current state of "paper" information used by managers, and to evaluate the prospects of moving that information to data processing supported medium. It is also recommended that assistants and secretaries be surveyed, so that they also feel like they are making important contributions to the system. The surveying process should be done carefully, so unwarranted fears of or resistance to the system are avoided. The mere announcement of a planned information system often triggers an immediate negative reaction from departments or managers who feel threatened by the new system.

5.2.2   Surveys

In almost all professional recommendations for building an information system, the first step is to determine the information need. This usually involves a survey of the eventual end users of the system. Most management consultants provide their clients with polished summary reports related to the surveys. The virtues of performing end user surveys before building an information system are also commonly extolled in university dissertation papers.

Don't Survey the End User

There is, however, reason to doubt that this is the most effective process for the initial development of an information system. Two major issues that need to be considered:

- End users tend to list their most pressing corporate responsibilities as their information needs during the project phase. For example, if a manager is being pressured to reduce inventory levels, that manager will push the system developers to emphasize detailed inventory monitoring displays. Or, if the price of raw materials is unstable during the project phase, managers are likely to list material price information as being critical. These examples show

how short-term pressures can take precedence over the true long-term needs of an information system.

- End user surveys often identify requests or desires that are impossible to achieve. Nothing is more difficult (or more frustrating) for the project group than the task of lowering unrealistic end user expectations. The end users will also grow frustrated, as they realize that their suggestions are not being built into the system. As their resentment grows, they may become less and less willing to accept the "inferior" system designed by the project group.

Alternative: Survey Employees

As a result of these concerns, there is a growing trend towards interviewing those employees responsible for processing and distributing corporate information. Instead of directly surveying end users, the system designers attempt to cull critical system success failures from the experiences and knowledge of employees who are familiar with the corporate "information culture". System designers can learn what data is available, and what data processing features are desired. They can also take advantage of these discussions to promote the new information system concept, and to quickly clear up any questions related to the new system. Also, if the corporate information suppliers buy into the system at an early stage, there is less risk of them viewing the new system as competition for scarce corporate resources and attention.

Suggest the Supply

Instead of relying on end user surveys, it is better to try to structure an information system driven by existing information, and information that can be reasonably (in terms of cost and effort) generated. Also, the information should be seen as important (or at least relevant) by the end users and the surveyed employees.

5.2.3   Topics

The division of information contents into system subject areas is a difficult but important task: While changing the end user application is easy to do, changing the structure of the underlying data is a complex and time-consuming procedure. A wide-ranging system design can prevent the development of parallel systems in individual subject areas. But it also requires that the system developers and administrators be capable of fulfilling the information needs of all the end users. Experience has shown how difficult it is to prepare useful information displays when corporate systems are not fully integrated with each other.

Wide-Reaching Information System Concept

Corporations should not be afraid to develop applications as part of a wide-reaching information system concept. Deadlines need to be set realistically, so that useful applications can be implemented in a time frame that is both acceptable to the end users and reasonable for developers. When developing a new system, it can be advantageous to set expected completion dates for portions of the systems as being three to five years after actual system development is planned to start. Such a clear message emphasizes the time and resources needed to create a flexible, functional system. Underestimating required resources is the most common cause for late system delivery. Neither the system sponsor nor the system developer are likely to have concrete experiences directly related to the project at hand, so there is a real danger that unrealistic implementation and performance expectations will arise. The people responsible for the system are very often lulled into making unrealistic promises about completion dates. Even if it is the unpopular position to take, it is better to err conservatively when estimating time requirements. Otherwise, the disappointment and dissatisfaction from the late system delivery can result in resentment towards and reluctance to use the system.

The process of choosing individual theme areas for an information system should not be driven by the software selected by the project managers. The SAP®-EIS program available today is simply not able to address all the reporting needs of a large corporation. Further, it is not a good idea to "save" important topics for future projects. General system plans should include all relevant corporate reporting needs, and should not be built around the limitations of popular hardware or software products. The following paragraphs illustrate how it is presently possible to build a more expansive system than would be possible using SAP®-EIS alone. The end user does not know if the data is retrieved from SAP®-EIS or some other information source. As far as the end user is concerned, it is irrelevant where the data is coming from, or what technology is used to get it to the desktop. The only thing that matters is the timely delivery of accurate information.

Possible topics include:

- Strategy
- Market/Exchange
- Business
- Organization
- Personnel
- Conclusions

Six Subjects per
Topic

For every topic, six subjects can be defined. Therefore, a total of 36 subject selections can be defined on the start-up sheet.

5.2.4   Themes

5.2.4.1   General Themes

Content
Responsibility

Themes are small, focused areas of expertise ("business objects"). The grouping of themes into topics is made according to the interests of the users. Whenever possible, editorial responsibilities should be assigned to the person or group responsible for system contents (see also page 166). Equally important is the ability to gather and process the necessary data within the defined schedules, without excessive time or money expenditures. The themes introduced here are not meant to be an exhaustive listing, but rather a stimulus to spur creative thinking on the part of the reader.

5.2.4.2   Strategic Area Themes

Portfolio Displays

This is an area for culling important strategic insights from the operative, service and central corporate areas. Portfolio displays are an example of strategic area representations; The most common portfolio displays are "profiles" and "amplifications." "Profiles" display a summary overview of the most important figures and results, while "amplifications" provide a detailed look at a particular situation in a particular business unit or area. The content and form of the display will vary from one company to the next, and will be strongly influenced by the industry or industries in which the company operates.

Investments

Another popular theme relates to investments. An example of this is a display of proposed increases in monthly investments over several regions or business units. The display can be further segmented by those increases that have been "approved," and those that are "planned." Yet another segmentation can be made to break out the individual projects in the regions or business units, etc. (see example page 134).

Research

Research plays a strategically important role in many companies. As such, it is not uncommon for companies to integrate research analysis into their strategic models. Creating a research theme further strengthens the information flow link from "defining research goals" to "launching research projects" to "project resolutions," and keeps upper management aware of this procession.

It is also a good idea to perform additional evaluations and alternative calculations (or simulations) with the data available in the strategic theme areas. These areas provide creative controllers with the ability to hone their present and future strategic decision-making skills. With the help of well-designed data repositories, the analyses can be made quickly and accurately.

5.2.4.3 Market/Exchange Area Themes

Market and stock exchange data are a good "add on" feature for an information system. It is now possible to pull this data from several different external services. In most cases, this data is automatically converted into a form recognizable by almost all information system application products. Some companies have created separate units that are responsible for processing such external data so that it can be displayed or analyzed in proprietary corporate information systems.

Competition

A comprehensive application should also have a theme devoted to competitor analysis. The screens in this theme area should compare quarterly as well as yearly results for both the company itself and its major competitors. The data should be as up-to-date as possible, so that accurate and meaningful comparisons can be made. Information from directly competing businesses in the same region are of particular interest. This information often already exists within the individual businesses, in a form that can be used by the information system applications. With very little effort, it should be possible to calculate consolidated results for competitors.

Raw Material Prices

The central marketing research department may have additional data related to countries, companies and business units that could be an advantageous supplement to the central information system themes areas.

Yet another theme should address the subject of raw material prices, especially in companies where these prices play a vital role in determining overall strategic goals. Commentaries, forecasts, and trends identifications enhance the purely numeric historical data, and help both operative and strategic managers to better run their departments/divisions.

Stock Market Information

The "Shareholder Value" concept places an added emphasis on a company's stock value. Taken to the extreme, one could argue this concept reduces a company's output to one single product, namely its stock shares. All other products, be they pharmaceuticals, plastics, chemicals or whatever, are merely tools for providing the necessary return on capital to investors. For this reason, many companies include a stock market (and currency market) theme in their information systems. These theme areas should contain current data (including price fluctuations in after-market transactions) and offer several different analysis perspectives. The analysis can be a simple timeline display, or as complicated as indexed comparisons and simulation models (see Styleguide Element "Index" on page 121).

Market Information Systems

Market information systems, which are often located within the various corporate entities, can provide data about customers and competitors that can be consolidated to provide additional strategic insights. These systems take on added value if many corporate entities are working in overlapping fields. This consolidation is not always possible, due to incompatible terminologies and structures in different businesses or departments. The ability to deliver such consolidated information should, however, be a goal of a modern information system.

5.2.4.4 Business Area Themes

This area displays controlling data for operative functions. The most important financial results like revenues, profits, cash flow return on investment (CfRoI) etc. can be analyzed in different "views." These include time analyses like monthly development, comparisons with previous years, or actual/budget comparisons. Further, the results can be viewed according to regional structures, subsidiary results, or division results. The contents in this theme area will depend on the nature of the corporation; corporations that are true world-wide operating concerns will require data displays that are different from those needed by a holding company that is only interested in acquiring and selling companies. It is not unusual for the parent company in a concern to be of central importance to senior management, to the extent that they desire daily displays relating to parent company sales, orders, and inventory. Very often these daily totals are not available at the corporate level, or at least they are not as accurate and reliable as the figures for the parent company alone.

Importance of Commentaries

In this typical EIS system theme area, drill-down technology is essential. Drilldowns enable system users to move deeper into the detailed data that drives the summarized corporate or subsidiary results. Even more important than drilldowns are data commentaries. Commentaries that explain significant variations, or point the user to possible trouble areas, move a system from merely reporting numeric results to providing real value-added insights.

The business area also includes data related to industry supply and demand. Whenever possible, this data should be displayed using the same structure as the sales and profit data display.

5.2.4.5   Organization Area Themes

Catch-All

A company's organization area can be a catch-all category for corporate issues that do not fit cleanly into the other defined system themes. For example, various organization plans would fall into this category, and additional information related to the implications of these plans could be included as well. The possible spectrum ranges from a simple telephone book to a detailed biographical display of board members, broken down by their involvement in the company's various subsidiaries. Attention should also be given to data related to specific corporate operating conditions, like accident statistics and environmental protection data. A further possibility is to use this theme area for displaying new government regulations, and to provide employees with access to "handbooks" outlining acceptable corporate behavior and operating guidelines.

Cost Data

Cost data is another popular theme. This is especially true for the parent company and the more important subsidiaries. This theme takes on an increased urgency when figures for the corporation as a whole are not available in a consolidated form. Many firms possess specific cost planning and budgeting data, which should be an essential part of an overall information system.

Very often, there is an interest in being able to view data about a company's world-wide sales and production programs. It is a good idea to create a separate system theme for this topic.

5.2.4.6 Personnel Area Themes

In today's rapidly changing business environment, personnel development is become more and more important. Companies still need access to pure "per head" figures, but they should also be able to access information related to the age, experience, and qualifications of employees. In light of the numerous ways of viewing personnel numbers, a system also needs to be able to display personnel data based on regional, functional, and organizational structures.

Time Management

Time management can be a separate system theme as well. This emphasizes the importance of monitoring where personnel resources are going, even though data concerning time activities may not be measured at every level of the corporation.

Extra Security for Sensitive Personnel Data

Top management information, like succession plans and candidate lists, is extremely sensitive and needs to be protected. The security issues do not disappear when the information is stored in an information system. A common problem for many companies is finding a technological solution that is completely effective at preventing outside or unauthorized system access (see page 180).

5.2.4.7 Decision Area Themes

It is difficult to "structuralize" a corporate decision-making process. This situation is exacerbated by the fact that much of the data needed to make important decisions is in an unstructured form. It is essential that the system have access to transcripts from important meetings, including minutes from board meetings and findings from expert committee studies. If the information system is to be more than an electronic storage bin, a great deal of thought and effort needs to be devoted to developing the final system structure. Technical resources alone are not enough. In the area of strategic decision-making, users need to have access to extensive editorial commentaries related to the raw data the system provides.

5.2.5

Newspapers Have
"Charm"

News

The concept of a "virtual corporate newspaper" is similar to that of an information system, if the newspaper is driven by the latest news available. Announcements from different press agencies (filtered and processed by an internal corporate system) can be displayed. The public relations division is often responsible for creating and maintaining a corporate newspaper. Since important announcements can be found in traditional media outlets on the following day, it makes sense to remove them from the virtual newspaper every evening. Newspapers listing around 15 announcements per day, ordered by their entry into the system, have proven to be most effective. Messages that are particularly important should be color-coded to distinguish them from less important announcements.

Displaying News on
the Start-up Sheet

It is best to position the news on the system start-up sheet, with the headlines listed under "Highlights". If a user clicks on a headline, the corresponding text entry will appear on the screen.

5.2.6

Identifying
Appointment
Changes

Appointments

A schedule administration program is typically a support function provided by the data processing department. It is important to draw a distinction between general and personal appointments. General appointments include regularly scheduled events like department meetings, project report meetings, and quarterly report press conferences. Changes in the scheduling of these events should be clearly recognizable (see the example on page 121).

A user must further decide which personal meetings and appointments to include in an appointment system. Few companies have clearly-defined guidelines for choosing personal appointment software programs. Usually, individual users can launch whatever personal administrator program they prefer, directly from the information system.

5.2.7

Integrating Various
Information Services

Communication

In a modern information system, it is impossible to ignore the necessity for communication components. Ideally, it should be possible to individually integrate the necessary software programs into the system. In addition to appointment administrator programs, the modern employee should have access to a fax, Email, external services like AOL and CompuServe (and, if accessible through the corporate network, the Internet). There is little doubt that the Internet will become more and more important to corporate communications in the future. The subject of appropriate corporate communication strategies is addressed later in this book (see page 155).

5.2.8   Personal Information

The ability to manage personal information (like meeting notes or project draft ideas) is an attractive performance feature in an information system. For such a feature to be used effectively, the system end users need to be comfortable and familiar with computers. Unfortunately, there are no programs available today that can be used to easily and reliably store and retrieve this kind of information. To be viable for widespread corporate usage, such a program would need to be able to catch logical errors input by users, and automatically correct these errors. A particularly interesting feature would be an intelligent link to the contents of the information system. But this type of software still appears to be years away from reaching the market.

5.3   Creating a Productive Data Warehouse

5.3.1   Data Model

Data Stored in
Normal Tables

When developing base data processing systems, the data model acts as the development "blueprint." In an information system this is not always the case: Based on the data in existing relational databases, value tables are defined for structured data. The key terms are then stored in register tables (= Normalizing, a relational processing theory designed to prevent data redundancy). It is rare that multiple value tables need to be accessed for a single information system display. Entities play a subordinate role in such cases. Very often, complete data models that incorporate the data from base data processing systems already exist. If this is the case, the data model must simply be expanded to include the necessary report tables.

5.3.2   Table Structure

Combining Different
Data Sources

SAP®-EIS only administers data related to the SAP business model. As an example, it is not possible to build a telephone directory based on the data in an SAP application. For the developer, this means that it will probably be necessary to link one or more further data sources to the information system. Regardless of how many external data sources are used, the SAP files remain the backbone of the information system. The ideal is to create a system stemming from multiple data sources, but accessed using a single user interface. It is then possible to display data that has nothing to do with (or is not yet incorporated into) the SAP family of systems.

SAP®-EIS stores its output data in relational tables. The first step in this process is the creation of so-called reports, which is a multidimensional data cube stored in the main memory of the server. SAP-GUI (Graphical User Interface) or inSight® is then used as a front-end to access and display data. Since SAP-GUI is designed more for controllers, and less for "normal users," this book focuses on information systems designed with inSight® as the front-end. inSight® makes it easy to create user interfaces that are comfortable to use and easy to administer.

OLAP, ROLAP

A hot subject among software developers today has to do with OLAP (On-line Analytical Processing, see page 7). The question is whether multidimensional information needs to be stored physically in a multidimensional structure, or if it is better to store the data relationally and to use virtual data cubes for data processing. The latter method is referred to as ROLAP (Relational OLAP). Both methods are achievable today, and in an ideal system they are combined with each other. In other words, the information system is stored in different "System Pieces." From the end user vantage point, "system pieces" are less than desirable if each piece requires its own user interface. A system that utilizes a single user interface across all system pieces is more likely to earn widespread acceptance. With a single user interface, the end user doesn't see the different system pieces, so he has the feeling that he is working with a single system. inSight® was designed to operate as a specialized "system piece organizer", providing managers with a user-friendly link to access and analyze information from various corporate data sources. inSight® enables fast application development and intelligent information handling, despite the fact that it is not equipped with any specialized data processing or analysis functions. Ideally, these operations should occur in the system level below the GUI. SAP®-EIS, whose reports structure data records according to the SAP system business concept, is an example of such a system.

Business Logic in
SAP®-EIS

SAP®-EIS offers considerable advantages over relational database solutions : SAP®-EIS delivers data already structured with a business logic (unlike in a relational database). The application developer is free to concentrate on building a user-friendly system, without having to worry about developing the system business logic. Direct SQL commands should be limited to business areas not (yet) built into SAP®-EIS.

Since there are a number of interesting topics related exclusively to relational databases, development with relational databases should not be ignored. The following section of this book addresses various methods that can help improve SQL query response times in inSight® applications.

5.3.2.1   Indexes

Better Performance
Through Indexes

The process of accessing data from a relational database table can be considerably improved through the use of indexes. An index "sorts" the attributes in a database column, so that the contents of that column aren't sequentially read during a query. When dealing with larger database tables, the skillful use indexes is a necessity for achieving good information system performance. After developing an inSight® application, it is a good idea to   identify the SQL commands that are most often generated, and define indexes accordingly. The CREATE SCRIPT functions are useful here, as they create files listing all the SQL queries sent during a given query session. During such a query session, it makes sense to use the screens and selections that are most likely to be used by end users. This insures that defined indexes correspond to the actual usage patterns of end users. In extreme cases, a well-defined index can reduce a query processing time from several minutes to a few seconds.

5.3.2.2   Summary Data

Pre-Calculated Sums

Like indexes, summary data is an important weapon in a system designer's arsenal. By developing an automated process where data sums are generated when raw data is fed into the system, it is possible to pull back query results without having to search the entire base table. The benefits of summary data are most visible in situations where a given query is executed on a regular basis. For example, the figure for a corporation's total monthly sales revenue is likely to be requested several hundred times over the course of a month. If the query is sent to the main data table every time, there will be a considerable burden on the database server. To reduce this load, and to improve the performance of the system, summary tables can be created (most multidimensional databases, in order to provide quick and accurate results, need to completely calculate results over the entire main table; with larger data sets, the calculation process can take several hours to complete).

Summary Rows Make Relational Tables Confusing

A special summary identification column describes the various summary rows. The advantages of being able to create more elegant database queries needs to be weighed against the element of confusion and clutter a summary row adds to a relational table. For this reason, the summary identification column entries are generated according to mathematical rules. This makes it possible for MIS applications to automatically generate direct SQL queries. A normal SQL query that does not ignore the summary row would result in a value much higher than the true value of the query, because it would add the summary row to the total. It can be more difficult to write queries with "normal" SQL tools; in some cases, it is impossible.

To be an effective tool for creating information systems in conjunction with relational databases, the tool must be able to properly handle summary rows. The inSight® tool meets this requirement.

Consolidation

Yet another advantage (which is sometimes a necessity) of working with summary rows occurs in situations where certain information can not be displayed by simply adding up the existing data records. This is often the case in calculating consolidated corporate results, where intra-company transactions are reported in the system. In such cases, the consolidated summary totals need to be calculated and entered into summary rows, instead of being processed by the data processing tools in the information system.

5.3.2.3

Summary Tables

Managers often find themselves in situations where they need a highly-summarized information display, one that combines miscellaneous information from a number of different sources. As an example, many companies use a "highlight" screen to display turnover and profit figures, inventory levels, pending orders, etc. for selected subsidiaries. This corporate overview is essential to monitoring and analyzing if corporate objectives are being met, and it requires the retrieval of data from a number of different databases and database tables. This data must then be processed and summarized, which can lead to extremely poor system performance. Slow applications are doomed to failure, as modern managers are unwilling and unable to waste valuable time waiting for screen displays to process.

The processing of screen displays is considerably faster if the various data records are combined into a separate, dedicated database table. The actual generation and calculation of the data records for this table can occur at night, so as not to interfere with the functioning of the operative systems.

5.3.2.4   Views

Access Privileges

Views (virtual extracts from relational databases) were not originally designed to facilitate better system performance. Their real purpose is to administer who has access to what data. Examples from real corporations have proven that the administration of (sometimes illogical) access privileges (or, perhaps better: access restrictions) make it harder to administer the information system as a whole. Developers need to plan both time and effort for resolving this situation.

Dynamic View Administration

Dynamic view technology can considerably reduce administrative efforts (assuming that the selected database system supports the technology). This technology causes the information system to query a view available to all system users. The catch is that the view is not filled until an actual query is generated by the system. When a query is generated, the data corresponding to the users access privileges is loaded into the view. User access privileges are defined in access tables stored in the database system. A common access table format is to use the company's organization plan; the user has access to the corporate data related to his position, and all his subordinate positions. By using the database system (instead of the MIS application) to regulate user access privileges, the risk of a user accessing restricted data with a separate SQL query tool is eliminated.

It is also possible to define explicit views for each individual system user. However, this strategy is not recommended except in cases where the generation of dynamic views leads to unacceptable system performance results.

5.3.3   Building Tables

5.3.3.1   Separate Tables

Administering Access
Privileges

In general, it is a good idea to create separate tables for the MIS if similar tables already exist elsewhere in the company. On the one hand, it is easier to set up user accounts and access privileges to the MIS's "own" data tables. On the other hand, it may be necessary to alter or modify data records within the system data tables (see also page 37). If creating separate tables is not an option, it is also possible to set up views of the "foreign" tables. The database system treats the views like real tables, but saves the work of creating copies of the original tables.

In databases, data is usually stored in a series of value tables. Texts related to the values are stored in central register files. Just as with value tables, a critical issue for register tables is whether or not they should be duplicated specifically for the information system. If they are duplicated, detail should be paid to insuring that the same table structures and field definitions are used, so that copy routines can be easily automated. Unfortunately, it is not always possible to avoid having to modify data or data structures in the duplicate system. One example is the need to divide entries in Lira by 1,000 if the database driver program otherwise makes errors in processing extremely large Lira values. In such cases, these "alterations" should be clearly and prominently documented.

5.3.3.2   SAP®-EIS Tables

Aspects

SAP®-EIS has its own database, which consists of multiple database tables. Each one of these tables groups related business data together, and has its own individual structure. In SAP®-EIS, each different data area is called an "aspect. " The aspects separate the EIS database into individual, independent from each other data areas. Possible data areas include contract identification codes, profit center information and additional market data. In addition to the database table, an aspect also consists of a structural description, screen layout, a user interface, and programs for collecting and displaying data. SAP supports the Oracle and Informix (to name a couple) database systems as a source for the aspect tables.

Characteristics and
Key Figures

An aspect consists of characteristics and key figures. Characteristics are descriptive terms like Industry, Region, Department or Firm. SAP refers to combinations of characteristic values (e.g. Industry: Pharmaceuticals, Region: New England) as analysis objects. The selection of characteristics and key figures during the definition of the SAP®-EIS determines the data analyses that are possible within the system.

5.3.3.3   SAP®-EIS Reports

Ad Hoc Analysis and
Briefing Books

Using the characteristics and key figures in an aspect, SAP®-EIS can generate Reports that can be used as the base for analyses performed by the two SAP®-EIS tools (ad hoc analysis and the briefing book). These Reports can also be directly accessed using inSight®, and the data they contain can be displayed in any inSight® layout format. The first time a Report is needed, it is immediately built as a virtual data cube in the server's main memory. The structure of Reports is based on the SAP business model. This can be seen as a huge advantage over systems using relational tables, where the business logic must somehow be built into the system. For example, SAP®-EIS data is automatically linked to the base data behind it, while in a relational model this link must be manually defined.

Combining With
Relational Tables

inSight® applications that link to SAP®-EIS reports are preferable to applications that link to relational tables. For areas not covered by SAP's business concept, links to relational tables are the only option. For simplicity's sake, one could store this additional data in the same database system that SAP®-EIS uses to store its aspects. Using inSight®, it is possible to simultaneously access SAP®-EIS reports and relational tables. Information from these two sources can be displayed in the same document, so the end user won't notice that the information is coming from multiple data sources.

5.3.3.4   Relational Databases

Extensive Experience

From a technical perspective, relational databases are an excellent data source for inSight®-based information systems. The positive experiences companies have had using inSight® and relational databases (through the appropriate ODBC interface) support this claim. The interface to SAP®-EIS reports was developed later than the ODBC interface, so it is difficult to make definitive statements about the SAP®- inSight® interface. This is, however, surely just a matter of time.

In the past, many firms centrally stored a large number of relational tables, which were periodically updated with data from the operative systems. Common tables used were related to turnover, profits, inventory, accounts payable, personnel, etc. These tables (and sometimes table extracts) were accessed by senior and middle managers as well as strategic employees in various business units. Due to the highly complex nature of relational tables, data queries were created by a limited number of specialists. Using relational data sources and a PC text processing or spreadsheet program, the specialists created paper reports for their individual business units. Values and displays were corrected as errors and updates came in (see page 37), and these corrections were sent directly to the central data tables. The logical consequence of all this is that different values related to the same topic often appeared at different levels of the company. The confusion and uncertainty this caused resulted in a considerable expenditure of time and personnel to determine the correct value.

Report Databases

On the other hand, the positive impact of "report database" development can not be ignored. These databases forced organizations to thoroughly analyze their information structures. Even if there is only a small group of specialists working on the content, the extensive use of these databases constantly puts pressure on the information providers to improve the quality and timeliness of raw data. Pressure from query specialists alone is not enough to guarantee continuous data improvement; query specialists are rarely able to influence corporate priorities, and their superiors aren't usually interested in addressing data quality issues. As a result, these "specialists" are forced to learn how to use other data processing tools, like the powerful PC programs that are now on the market. If the end users were actually using data from the original tables, there would probably be more pressure to improve data quality, and subsequently the quality of the analyses made with the data.

Linking Employees to the New Information Concept

As a first attempt at creating an information system, like building a prototype, it makes sense to use these tables. Developers should be careful not to develop "better" parallel data sources. This would only lead to crippling corporate conflict and in-fighting. It would also endanger the support of the people responsible for distributing corporate information; if these people do not feel responsible for the success of the project, the very survival of the new information concept is threatened (see page 81).

Structured Query Language

Retrieving information from relational databases is done using the database language SQL (Structured Query Language). inSight® applications are designed to automatically generate the appropriate SQL commands. inSight®'s query generator is extremely flexible, so there is no need to customize the program to work with different databases or database tables. As an example, it is possible to use month labels as column headings, or to retrieve them for display as entries in a display table. Automatically generating queries over combination keys isn't a problem, nor is it a problem to create queries for sum entries. As a result, queries of larger relational database tables can be retrieved within acceptable time parameters. A particularly noteworthy feature of inSight® is the ability to make data queries and data entries **using a single application**. This makes the process of creating entire read/write systems possible and easy. Many competitive products can not offer such a feature. Care should be taken in designing systems that allow user database entries, as many databases lack adequate control mechanisms for table entries. This is especially true in systems that allow for distributed input. As an example, the use of ODBC with IBM's DB2 database is only possible with dynamic SQL (instead of static SQL, where the server "recognizes" and controls database entries).

Cascade Query

There is another obvious requirement that many query tools on the market today fail to fulfill. As direct descendants of report generation tools, many query tools are only able to send one SQL statement per query. This contrasts with the needs of conventional display tables, where multiple queries need to be sent to retrieve all the necessary data. Imagine a table with a "Current_Budget" display heading, and another table entry is used to identify the month for which the budget figures are valid. At some point during the year, new budget data will replace the older budget data, and the valid month entry in the table is updated. The old data records from the "Current_Budget" column will be transferred to the "Old_Budget" column. If the task of administering and understanding the budget updates is to be automated rather than left to the system users, the application must contain additional "orientation" queries that guide the user to the data he or she is looking for (when accessing data from SAP®-EIS reports, this process becomes superfluous).

When dealing with larger relational tables, the use of complex systems of queries can lead to unacceptable system performance. The "normal" query response time for an information system should lie between three and eight seconds. Generally speaking, system performance can be improved by creating targeted indexes (see page 91) on individual columns or combinations of columns. If indexes are not effective, system designers should consider using summary data (see page 91). This means presumming higher-level data into separate tables, so the data can be retrieved in a more timely fashion. In extreme cases, a designer can resort to data extracts or even new tables containing data from multiple other tables (see page 92). By drastically improving system performance, the system designer can significantly increase the likelihood of widespread end user acceptance.

5.3.3.5   Tables for HTML Information

Classical management information systems are usually limited to displaying structured information. As a result, the MIS variations like LIS (Leadership Information System), DSS (Decision Support System) or EIS (Executive Information System) often provide analysis of the same data, albeit at different hierarchical levels: turnover and results by period, comparisons with budget and previous year results, and results broken down by sales region, business unit, or some other organizational structure. Software companies have developed advanced drill-down technologies, enabling the user to analyze the various dimensions of the "data cube" from virtually any perspective. This trend seems to have little to do with the actual needs of today's managers. Although drill-down technologies provide software companies with interesting marketing possibilities, experience has shown that managers quickly lose interest in what often amounts to a "needle in the haystack" search method. The average manager prefers to have an assistant or analyst provide information related to variations from plan or noteworthy results. As a result, powerful drill-down possibilities usually end up in presentations or demo models, and not in the actual MIS systems used by managers.

Drill-down Technology

The reasoning behind managerial reluctance to accept and use drill-down technologies is simple; most managers don't believe it is part of their job to search for information, even if the data is stored in convenient electronic data cubes. There is an initial excitement to being able to view data from all the different hierarchical business levels. But once a manager has seen all these levels, the interest quickly subsides. Even with today's technologies, searching for data in a large data repository is a boring process. Very often, apparent variations in corporate data are not indicative of variations in market conditions. Instead, they often reflect special bookkeeping or data entry tricks, which are of absolutely no interest to a manager. The traffic light graph, highly-praised as the ideal exception reporting indicator, has also had problems establishing itself as a corporate norm. Cynics have compared the optical display of a traffic light graph to an "over-decorated Christmas tree."

Electronic Newspaper

The concept of an electronic newspaper has proven to be a more popular option. An electronic newspaper contains a brief listing of important subjects in headline form on the start-up sheet, from which the user can call up more detailed information on any of the listed subjects. Users can still access other elements of the corporate data archives, but the emphasis of the system is on delivering relevant, current information.

Unstructured Information

To successfully implement an electronic newspaper concept, there must be some possibility for displaying unstructured information (i.e. formatted texts, pictures, etc.). Raw numeric displays and unformatted texts aren't "sexy" enough to hold user interest. In the past, there was no general standard for processing unstructured information. The problem is twofold: The technology is too new, and too few editorial powers from the print and television fields have realized the importance of this subject. Neither Lotus Notes nor the PDF format from Adobe, to name two examples, have been able to achieve a decisive breakthrough in this field. They are simply too complex for an information system. On the other side, Microsoft with its OLE technology and APPLE (together with other software companies) with its Opendoc concept prevented the corporate world from accepting either as a unified standard. APPLE and IBM have recently abandoned the Opendoc concept. IBM, along with three other firms, has decided to adopt JavaBeans as their unstructured information concept.

Enormous Growth in Popularity of Internet

HTML technology, which has played a major role in the growing popularity of the Internet, appears to be the first real acceptable standard for processing unstructured information. The major advantages to HTML are its user-friendliness (both for developers and end users), and its cross-platform capabilities. HTML delivered what software and hardware providers had unsuccessfully promised for years: the ability to pull all levels of society into the electronic information landscape.

Corporate Home Page

Most internal corporate Internet systems (called "Intranets") lack a comfortable and appealing link to the data stored within it. The key to creating this user-friendly link to the data is the corporate home page, from which users can move to any of the individual divisions' or companies' web pages. When viewing existing home pages, one often has the impression that the division or company only has an Intranet web page so they can claim to be "progressive." These pages usually contain the infamous "Who we are" information, which a visitor may view once and then never again. There has not (yet) been a system designed that informs users where important information can be found within an Intranet, and how reliable that information is. Search machines are commonly used to fill this information gap, but the success of this technique remains questionable. The worst case scenario is that the Intranet degenerates into a collection of hundreds of individual home pages, whose contents are less than informative and are rarely viewed. It is valid to note that, even in this worst case scenario, there is no concrete damage done to the company or its employees. However, it is also valid to point out the total lack of corporate benefits from such a scenario would argue against simply implementing HTML technology for the sake of it.

An advantage of storing information in relational database tables is the clear overview of the data it provides: The contents of the tables can be used to efficiently navigate through the information in the system. The inSight® applications described in this book are based on using data from relational database tables; the ease with which information navigation objects like menu objects and radio button objects (see page 58) can be filled with contents from the database tables is the point that needs to be stressed here. Databases also offer powerful system administration tools, so that it is easier to monitor and maintain massive numbers of data records.

No HTML Administration Tools

In contrast to this, there are no proven tools available for administering HTML information. Data-driven navigation is also more difficult with HTML. Currently, navigation is done primarily through "links," which are static and operate only in a linear fashion. Dynamic navigation, like probing the detailed data behind a certain numeric result, can only be accomplished through complex Java programming. What could be more obvious than using database tables to administer HTML objects and to control navigation within the information system applications?

HTML Objects in inSight®

The link between the HTML pages on a web server and the actual information tables themselves is the URL address. The URL address identifies the physical location of the HTML page. The URL can be stored in a database and retrieved using inSight®. When this technique is used, inSight® displays the HTML page in a document object, just like if it were data from a relational table.

This process is completely invisible to the user: there is no way for the user to know if information is coming from a relational table, or from an SAP®-EIS Report, or from an Internet/Intranet web server. The only thing that the user knows is that the information is current and reliable. The information system administrators are responsible for guaranteeing this last point.

A data record describing an HTML information entry could appear as follows:

- Administrative Section:
  - HTML document number
  - Document name
  - Anchor point, if necessary
  - Author
  - Content administrator
  - Creation date
  - Date of last change
  - URL address

- Control Section:
  - Topic
  - Subject
  - Area of expertise
  - Description
  - Highlight (one line description that can be used on the start-up sheet of the corporate electronic newspaper)
  - Date highlight was published

- Date highlight was deleted
- Subscriber groups (for "different" newspaper layouts)

Unified Corporate
Structure

It is a good idea to define a unified corporate-wide meta data structure. Such a structure makes it easier to use the HTML information to pool data into an information reservoir for various applications used in the company.

Navigation through
the Database

One of the advantages of HTML technology, namely hyperlink navigation, may actually prove to be a hindrance to managing an efficient information system. This is because the static references it uses can be very difficult to maintain and update. For this reason, it is a good idea to use as much database-supported navigation in an information system as is possible.

5.3.4   Meta Data

Meta data has an important role in the Data Warehouse concept. Meta data is basically the system's "information about the information." This includes a definitive catalog of terms. Ideally, the catalog of terms also includes definitions from the operational business environment.

The original meta data concept was to provide end users with an overview and entry point for interacting with the information system. Together with so-called query tools (which automatically generate SQL queries), meta data would help end users efficiently organize their contact with the Data Warehouse. The concept has proven to be a valuable one, although it has been much more successful with controllers and assistants (i.e. the people who prepare information for the end users) than with the actual end users themselves. The reason for this is the fact that, in order to effectively create information system applications, the user must have a sound understanding of the often complex table structures within the information system. It is unrealistic to expect high-ranking managers to spend time learning these structures, but it is very realistic to delegate this task to an assistant or controller.

New Definition of
Meta Data

At this point, it makes sense to develop a new definition for "meta data." The initial tenets according to which the Data Warehouse and OLAP pioneers operated, namely that the data processing department "does not need to consider the wants of the end users" (see page 7), are no longer valid or justifiable. Meta data does not even come close to fulfilling the goal of providing end users with access to and an understanding of the information system table structures. The true importance of meta data can be found on the technical side of the information system: It helps the developer build an efficient information system. The benefits to the end users are indirect benefits, i.e. they manifest themselves in the end user application interface. Meta data that is created through the use of classical Data Warehouse tools should therefore remain invisible (or perhaps transparent) to the ultimate system end users.

Business Object
Repository

Another important function of meta data is to facilitate the development of a business object repository for an information system. The business object repository does not need to be defined at the start of system development; instead, it should grow in conjunction with the growth of the total information system. Seasoned project leaders and sponsors comment over and over about the importance of having something "usable" to show users. Otherwise, support and resources for the project may dwindle. Long project preparation phases, even if they are used to build a valuable core meta data resource, should be avoided. But in the end it is up to the project group (and project leader) to decide on the direction of the information system. Unique corporate requirements, infrastructure, and the macroeconomic situation as a whole will surely play a significant role in shaping information system development.

5.3.5   Help Programs

Building an information system for a large German corporation was an enlightening experience. The system has been in operation for over three years, but it is continuously modified and updated. The number of help files the system requires were considerably underestimated when the project began. The trials and tribulations associated with the project make it clear why there is no "ready-to-use" Data Warehouse on the market. Most of the help files are related to copy processes. Some deal with processes executed on a regular basis (i.e. every night), while others are executed every time new data is entered into the system. The task of controlling and administering the data in an information system is a significant responsibility, albeit one that can be partially automated with suitable software programs.

The "Application Administration" section on page 150 addresses this subject in more detail.

5.3.6 Documentation

Extensive Docu-
mentation

Documentation for a Data Warehouse and the related information system can quickly grow to be as large as the actual application. This is especially true in cases where individual user
settings are included in the documentation. The major benefit of
centrally storing user dependent application settings is that these
settings can then be accessed from any PC linked to the system.
The subject of documentation is addressed in more detail starting
on page 177.

5.4 Creating a Prototype

5.4.1 Concept

5.4.1.1 Organization

Once the decision to develop a prototype has been made, those
responsible for the project need to quickly define the resources
and organizational requirements for building and maintaining the
information system. The information system itself is not capable
of creating the information it is designed to display. Information
needs to come from the various departments and divisions
within the company, in as "clean" and usable a form as is possible. When management decides to build an information system
spanning broad strategic and operative areas of the company,
they often realize that the desired information is already available: The difficult task is then to integrate all these different data
records and formats into a single system. The areas providing the
raw data usually feel that there is nothing wrong with their conventional data format. In many cases, they will vehemently de-
fend the status quo data form, out of a fear of losing power,
influence, and responsibility to the data processing department.
This scenario does occur in some cases, but there are also other
"threats" to the power and status of a corporate division. As an
example, technological advances are constantly forcing companies to replace familiar and reliable data processing routines with
more competitive or cost efficient systems. But the benefits offered by the new systems, especially a centralized information
system, far outweigh the perceived disadvantages to the individual divisions and departments.

Convince the Data
Deliverers

Good internal marketing of the system is absolutely crucial in the early system development stages, to allay fears and misconceptions that may appear in individual divisions. It is not unusual for the various divisions within a company to operate under an uneasy truce with each other. In such cases, building a corporate-wide system that enjoys corporate-wide support is a daunting challenge.

Common Platform

A prototype can not be limited to the testing of technological solutions, but must also address organizational issues that the system will encounter. A convincing argument is that the information system should not be thought of as a conventional system. Instead, it is a common platform for processing, analyzing, and displaying information throughout the corporation. Individual divisions maintain the power to determine the contents and form of their own displays; the only new obligation is to conform to the uniform organizational and technical requirements of the new information system.

In the interest of future success, the architects of an information system need to guard against giving the impression that they will take over responsibility for the content of the information system. If the current information suppliers and data processors feel that their traditional information structures are being undermined, and their power is threatened, they are likely to resist the testing and implementation of the new system.

Project Responsibility

The situation can become tricky and complicated if responsibility for developing the new system is given to an area that is also charged with supplying some of the system's information content, like the controlling department. While there are advantages to having experienced employees from a related department handle the project, there are also some major disadvantages. Bruised egos often prevent other departments from fully cooperating in the system development. And the system itself may become too focused on areas and themes that are disproportionately weighted towards the reporting needs of the department developing the system. This can make it difficult if not impossible to later integrate additional theme areas that the system should be analyzing. Even the data processing department recognizes that they are not the appropriate department for establishing a conceptual structure for the project; they understand that their job is to store and process the system's data. Their experience in handling data is useless when it comes to defining the business logic and informal business processes that must be incorporated into the system.

Leading the Project Group

If there is nobody with detailed development experience available to head the project team, it is a good idea to appoint a leader who has no direct stake (i.e. political loyalties) in the development of the system. It is easier for a "neutral" project leader to build a project team out of employees from the functional departments and the data processing department. With the commencement of work on a prototype, or at the very latest with the launch of true on-line application development, the project team should have moved to a linear organizational structure. Ideally, the person responsible for running and maintaining the system will be one of the project team members. If that person is a controller or analyst, it makes sense to consider moving that person to the data processing department. Conversely, if that person is a computer specialist, it makes sense to consider transferring that person to one of the functional departments. Such a move has educational and experience benefits for the project leader, and it also makes it easier to integrate the interests of all these corporate areas into the project.

5.4.1.2 Technology

Abundance of Software Solutions

Many companies today, most notably larger ones, are attempting to limit the number of technical variations available within an information system. The ideal case is a system that runs on a single, corporate-wide technology solution. Because the larger, better known software companies have yet to bring a convincing information system solution to the market (many do not even use their own product), firms are looking to smaller and medium-sized software houses. Unfortunately, the market is currently flooded with products that claim to be the flexible information system solution for all situations. The use of SAP®-EIS in conjunction with the inSight® user interface will hopefully provide a benchmark for this market segment, clearing up the otherwise garbled discussion of what a software package can and should offer.

For corporations competing in the global arena, this is a development that can not come soon enough. Because the various business units are operating internationally, there is a very real danger that each business unit will select an information system framework that they feel is the "best fit" for their particular situation. Many companies lack both the financial and personnel resources needed to maintain multiple business unit-specific information systems, each with its own technical requirements. The only affordable solution is a standard system that can be applied across all business units. In this sense, it can only be viewed as positive if SAP is defining the standard, as they are the market leader for standard software in the business field.

Standardized Technology

A data processing-supported information system prototype should consider all these factors. In addition, it should adhere as closely as possible to a unified, standardized, corporate information system technology. Using SAP®-EIS is not a complete solution, because the software is not yet able to fulfill all the information and reporting needs of a modern corporation. It should serve as the framework for the system, and supplementary software packages should be chosen at least partially based on their compatibility with SAP®-EIS. Likely sources of additional data include relational databases and Internet/Intranet web servers. The inSight® user interface program is an ideal partner for such hybrid data sources, because it can combine data displays from all of these sources in a single document. Aside from having to enter the necessary passwords, the end user will have no idea that the data being displayed stems from multiple data sources. It is not even necessary to have SAP®-EIS up and running during the prototyping, even if the final system is intended to be SAP-based. A prototype running off a relational database can be expanded to include data from SAP®-EIS, or can use SAP®-EIS to completely replace the relational database at any time. This feature is particularly useful for companies that find themselves in the initial stages of SAP deployment. The deployment process can last up to several years, so it is important that the information system structure chosen be flexible enough to adapt to different development and operating environments.

International Standardization

For foreign companies with large US subsidiaries, the problem of adopting a standard information system for the entire corporation is extremely difficult. While the parent company may be working together with a native company to develop programs and applications, the US subsidiary is flirting with more established software companies who have newer and more tested products. The number of Data Warehouse, OLAP, and MIS software programs available in the US is unbelievably large. It is difficult even for industry experts to keep up with new product releases and existing product upgrades. An additional hurdle for inSight® is the fact that arcplan did not have a presence in the US until April 1997, and its market recognition is limited almost exclusively to companies that use the product in association with SAP.

In light of this reality, SAP's marketing strategy promoting the use of inSight® as a tool for expanding the capabilities of SAP® R/3 carries some significant weight. SAP favors this solution over other third party products because inSight® is the only product that can directly access the data in SAP®-EIS Reports; other products need to pull data from the aspect database tables, whereby the business logic in SAP®-EIS is lost. When a product directly interfaces to the aspect database tables, this business logic must somehow be programmed into the system being developed. While it is possible to build a system in this manner, the long-term prospects of maintaining, modifying and expanding such a system make it an untenable proposition.

5.4.1.3   Multilingual Capabilities

One of the goals of the design and development of a prototype is to investigate the feasibility of developing a larger information system. Creating a multilingual system (or at least a bilingual system with English as one language) is a good test for a prototype, and it can also contribute significantly to the international acceptance of the project.

Although SAP®-EIS is a true multilingual development tool, care must still be given to this issue. It is likely that the inSight® application will contain additional terms that do not originate in SAP®-EIS. Examples include the titles of user documents or the labels on navigation buttons (see example page 127).

Multilingual Tables of
Terms
This goal can be achieved if multilingual tables of terms are created before or during prototype development. The application can then be designed in a manner that causes the application to reference these tables before generating the document display.

5.4.1.4   Availability of Data

During the development of a prototype, data storage is not one of the more critical issues. Often times, sample data is simply stored locally (i.e. on the PC). Questions about data availability will eventually be raised, however, at the very latest when the prototype is presented to an end user or data processing employee. Any option that can not be built using existing or planned data processing resources can be automatically classified as an unattractive option. It is safe to assume that the existing data processing infrastructure will not be changed to accommodate a proposed new information system. As an example, the philosophy of creating a separate information system for the board of directors (with a separate network and dedicated server) was abandoned when the project was expanded to include key business unit executives. In contrast to the board members, who were all grouped together in the same building, the business unit leaders were spread all over the corporate campus. Some of the business unit leaders already had PCs, and had been integrated into the corporate network. The proposal to run a second line just for this system was quickly rejected due to logistical considerations. Despite the popularity of the system among the end users, the ultimate demise of the system was plain to see, mainly because the information system only ran on APPLE Macintosh computers. Today, the system data is stored on a central computer which is accessible to board members and key business unit executives via the corporate network. And, since inSight® was chosen as the application software, applications can be run on either Windows or Macintosh computers.

5.4.1.5   Mobility

Because many managers spend a great deal of time away from the office (and away from direct access to the corporate network), mobile system usage is a hot subject in many corporations today (see also page 25). A distinction needs to be made between external access and the temporary storage of selected data records. Both of these variations have advantages and disadvantages: While the former allows access to any and all data records in the system, the latter does not require a "connection" to the central system. It can thus be used in a taxi, at an airport, in an airplane, etc.

Access Over the Telephone or Internet

Theoretically, the system can be externally accessed over a telephone line or the Internet. In reality, most data processing personnel passionately object to the security risks associated with external access to proprietary systems. They prefer technically difficult solutions like call-back computer interfaces, where an interface can only be created when the call-back computer itself dials the number left by the traveling manager. This process is annoying and frustrating for users who want to access the system from a hotel room. A very good solution to the identification problem is the SecurID card, which displays a six digit security number that changes every couple of minutes. This number is synchronized with the central computer, and, since it can only be used once, there is no danger of non-authorized people exploiting the code. The system security can be further enhanced through the use of individual user PIN codes, so the system can not be breached even if a card is lost. This is a secure technology for mobile access, and appears destined for acceptance and use over the Internet in the very near future.

Building a local data repository (i.e. one that is stored on the hard drive of a portable PC) ignores the risks associated with unauthorized access to that PC. For example, who would have access to sensitive and/or confidential data if the PC were stolen, or if the hard drive had to be replaced due to a technical defect? For this type of mobile technology to be embraced, steps must be taken to insure that unauthorized users are unable to access the data on the PC. A basic security measure is requiring the user to enter a password when the computer is first started. Like most comparable systems, SAP®-EIS is not designed to allow direct local access to individual information blocks. Instead, it operates locally by retrieving data stored in files for programs like MS Excel® or MS Word®. This is neither an elegant nor a desirable solution to the problem. A new feature of inSight® is the ability to easily define and prepare selected data extracts for use in a mobile computing environment. However, it should be noted that there is not a lot of practical experience with this new technology. One of the problems that has yet to be solved is how to automatically delete the local data once it is no longer needed. If this problem is not addressed, there is no way to insure that relevant and current information is centrally (and safely) stored, in such a way that the portable users know that the displays they are viewing are also relevant and current.

Wireless Access Is Still Untested

The feasibility of using wireless access (like the MODACOM system) is an interesting but unproven possibility. There aren't enough of these products on the market, and existing products haven't been tested enough in real business applications to draw any significant conclusions.

5.4.1.6

Local Temporary Storage

Discussions about Data Warehouses almost always lead to users demanding that segments of the system data be stored on local servers. The term Data Mart (see page 2) is commonly heard in these discussions. For a corporate information system, the question becomes how to store the same data on multiple servers at the same time. New data storage and data processing issues always arise, because the complexity of storing corporate data has been increased. Data replication and data copying technologies should only be employed when the particular situation truly merits this step. An example would be a scenario where PCs were unable to connect to the central server.

5.4.2   Information Sources

5.4.2.1

Internal Information Sources

Most managers get the majority of their written information from paper sources. Reading articles and data displays from electronic information sources remains the exception rather than the rule. Internet web servers are still no competition for a well-designed information system, because of the time needed to actually find useful data. Also, the distractions of advertisements and the tendency of companies to put their own spin on displayed information sometimes makes Internet information less reliable than information from a known and trusted traditional source.

Other Presentation
Forms are Possible

It is not an easy task for information providers to make the jump from paper display to computer monitor display, because the range of technological possibilities is so immense. A dynamic user interface enables users to access a much broader information base than is possible with any paper medium. The backside of this new technology is the difficulty of controlling and ordering the system contents. Information ordering and control is much easier with paper displays, because assistants or controllers can simply print out the displays requested by their superiors, and then wait for the next information request.

Data Infrastructure

In addition to the content issue, there is also a technical component that needs to be considered: To implement an information system for processing electronic data requests, a company must create a suitable data infrastructure. In the past couple of years, the term "Data Warehouse" has been developed to describe such an infrastructure (see Glossary page 197). This terms conjures up images of a system that provides easy access to whatever data is needed by whatever users, via any of the numerous query tools on the market today. In reality, despite numerous attempts to design and implement such systems, one is hard-pressed to find an example of an effective, operational Data Warehouse in a large corporation. The reasons behind this lack of success can be traced to the complex data processing issues involved, which managers can not and should not have to overcome. Unfortunately, there are no viable alternatives to a Data Warehouse as a basis for a corporate information system. As a matter of fact, no corporate-wide information system can hope to enjoy continued success without the support of a logically-ordered data infrastructure.

Appropriate Internal Information Sources

Usually, the search for appropriate internal information sources quickly reveals the need to build Data Warehouse structures. In addition to this technical issue, the actual data that is available is often not cumulated, unprocessed, commentary-free, and of generally poor quality. Thus, the task of cumulating, processing, and commenting on data in paper reports falls to knowledgeable analysts, whose "know-how" makes them literally irreplaceable. Sometimes, a new electronic information system will be introduced to run parallel to an existing paper reporting system. In such cases, the paper reporting system usually prevails, because users are familiar and comfortable with its structures. Serious efforts need to be made to insure that electronic systems are not viewed as "competitive" systems. Otherwise, it is likely that both information providers and users will allow the electronic system to wither on the vine.

Migration to SAP

Many firms are now planning on replacing their internally-developed legacy systems with standard software like SAP. As communication across different functional departments becomes more important, systems that integrate operational data in a unified data structure (like SAP) are becoming very popular. While standard software can solve many problems related to data analysis across different functional areas, it would be too optimistic to assume that these packages can also seamlessly integrate corporate logistics and information systems.

Transferring
Operative Data into
an Information
System

Operative systems are ideal for supporting logistical processes like order entry, product manufacturing, product storage, order shipping and billing. The data in operative systems is meant to monitor and facilitate the logistical processes, not to be gathered, processed, and analyzed in a business context by upper management. As a consequence of this, some operative data may not be an appropriate source of data for an information system. If it is used in analysis systems, it may be wrongly interpreted and could lead to incorrect decisions by management. If all the examples of companies falling into this trap were listed here, this book would have to be released in volumes. A number of these cases can be classified as examples of failing to make "Meaningful Comparisons" (see page 43).

Management by the
Plant Foreman

Even a subject as basic as allocating manufacturing costs is open to interpretation and debate. Production areas tend to use actual costs (i.e. full cost models), while sales and service areas prefer using calculated values (i.e. standard costs). When broken down to an individual product level, the variations in these two costing systems can be significant. From a sales perspective, the full cost system has the fatal flaw of being dependent on plant capacity usage ("Management by the plant foreman?"). The variable cost implications of the full cost system make it difficult to set pricing levels for ongoing customers.

Costing issues are a problem all the way to the total production costs and finance department level. There is an inherent conflict between the operational goals (accurately assessing the total production costs to maximize plant efficiencies) and the financial goals (using accounting standards to provide maximum shareholder value).

Different Points of
View

Depending on the overall corporate strategy, or on the department in which an executive works, the prevailing point of view is either correct or incorrect. This discussion is not intended to persuade corporations that one point of view is better than another. Instead, it is intended to illustrate some of the consequences of decisions made regarding the "view" of the data in an information system. Also, system designers need to be aware of the dangers of simply using unprocessed operating data as the system's data source. To this point, no corporation has successfully (and publicly) integrated two or more different cost or profit points of view into a system.

Failed Data Entry
Attempts

Attempts to manually input additional base data often result in incorrect data records hiding in the system. Even required entry fields are no guarantee that a system's more "informal" data will be input with the same care and quality control as the data coming directly from the operative systems. If an employee enters an incorrect product number or delivery amount, the error is easy to trace and the employee can be cautioned or reprimanded. However, if the same employee enters incorrect informal data, the likelihood of disciplinary repercussions is low. In many companies, there is no formal mechanism for checking the accuracy of informal data. The data ends up in a large file, where it is cumulated and displayed to end users in consolidated form. From a statistical perspective, the total margin of error is rarely significant at higher hierarchical levels, so the data displayed is generally reliable. But this is not necessarily true at lower hierarchical levels, and it can present real problems when individual data records are used for analysis. Users are quick to use the term "garbage data" to describe such data, even though it may be that only 1 % of the data is incorrect. The users do not know which 1% of the data is wrong, so they lose faith in the entire system. It is therefore important to insure that informal logistics level entries are subject to periodic quality and accuracy controls. The problem is that, from an economic perspective, the costs of these additional control procedures are too high to justify.

5.4.2.2

External Information Sources

External information should definitely have a role in a comprehensive information system. The system developers face the daunting task of deciding whether or not external data needs to be modified or processed in any way before it can be loaded into the system. If the data does need to be "touched up," a decision must be made as to who is responsible for processing the data. The obvious choices here are the system administrators themselves, or other internal departments with expert knowledge related to the specific data in question.

Information
Preparation by
Expert Departmental
Employees

It is not a bad idea to delegate responsibility for external information out to functional employees in relevant departments (marketing, finance, etc.). The public relations department can be responsible for current news, market research employees can handle data for overall market conditions, and the finance department is well-equipped to prepare stock and currency information. Farming out responsibility is a logical extension of the fact that these departments are already responsible for intra-corporate reporting in these areas. Another argument in favor of delegating responsibility is that these departments have the experts who are best-qualified to interpret and comment on the external information. Once this decision has been made, the challenge becomes motivating these departments to structure the information in such a way that it is compatible with corporate data processing infrastructures. The challenge can be particularly problematic in departments that already work with their own PC-supported information structures; if the key terms and codes they use differ from the corporate terms and codes, they need to be converted to match the central standards.

The process of standardizing terms and codes must revolve around creating a "clean" data processing structure. This task often expands beyond the capabilities of the departmental experts, who are reluctant to go through the whole process because they fail to see direct benefits for themselves and their departments. As a result, the conversion process can consume vast amounts of time and other resources, undermining managers' support for the system. One effective way of selling the conversion process is to identify and promote the ancillary benefits of the procedure for the specific department in question. Ideally, the system concept should include input from both the data processing department and the other functional departments. This enables the non-data processing employees to directly process and comment on the external data, while insuring that the data is in a form that is compatible with the overall information system structures.

5.4.3   Building Applications

5.4.3.1   Styleguide Elements

5.4.3.1.1   Layout

Layout Design
Handicaps

In general, not enough attention is paid to selecting an overall layout for an information system. On the one side, software firms have traditionally gone to market with less than impressive layout options in their programs. On the other, internal layout specialists (like employees in the advertising/marketing department) are experienced only in traditional mediums like paper displays. They are not familiar with the navigation possibilities software programs offer, and are therefore not qualified to fully exploit information system display possibilities.

This does not mean that these departments should be excluded from overall system layout planning. Their input can be crucial to integrating the corporate identity into whatever system gets developed. The offices of the top managers in most large corporations are distinguished from the offices of other employees by a tasteful (and expensive) decor. If an information system is to win the acceptance of these top managers, it too must be tastefully designed (in an optical sense). Most MIS user interfaces fail this test miserably. Interfaces created using inSight® and the input of layout specialists have received widespread praise from all levels of corporate users. Years of real-world testing and experimentation has reinforced the value assigned to designing an optically-refined layout.

Corporate Logo

Every company is responsible for deciding what Styleguide elements they wish to adopt as corporate standards. Things like screen background colors, the bordering styles around document objects, etc. should be standardized and applied consistently throughout company applications. Another consideration is whether or not to display the firm logo on every screen. Some application developers use an almost transparent version of the corporate logo as a background image on every screen. The important thing is that the formatting possibilities be used to create tasteful, consistent application screen layouts.

The User Should not
Notice System-
Specific Operating
Procedures

Equally as important as the layout is the method of navigation within an application. An information system has a good navigation system if the user is unaware of the system-specific operating procedure. The system should truly be a self-explanatory system. If it is not, it will be more difficult for the system to gain widespread acceptance. Many other media outlets have been successful for a long time because they are self-explanatory. Newspapers are a good example, as is the relatively new (but very user-friendly) video text. The user interface entices novice users, the information is current, and it is hard to find the same information in the same form in any other media outlet. It is not fair to directly compare a corporate-wide information system with newspapers and video text, but the information system should attempt to emulate their success strategies in as far as that is possible.

SVGA Standard

The SVGA standard of 800 x 600 is recommended for screen display. The display possibilities offer many advantages over the much smaller 640 x 480 VGA standard. The SVGA screen setting is now available on notebook computers for a reasonable price. Reasonably-priced portable SVGA projectors can be found on the market as well.

5.4.3.1.2   Interface Elements

To make the system friendly and inviting, the need to use the keyboard should be limited. In an ideal system, the only time the keyboard is needed is to type in user names and passwords when logging into different data sources. The users should be able to navigate through the rest of the system using nothing but the left mouse button. Double-clicks should be avoided if possible, because users can become confused and use double-clicks even where a single click would suffice. Similarly, users become confused when they constantly need to jump between left and right mouse clicks to operate the system. Instead of incorporating help text objects (or links to help text documents) into display documents, status line texts can be used: When the cursor is dragged over an object like a title, table, picture or graph, a descriptive text related specifically to the object appears in the document's status line (in the lower left-hand corner of the document). The text is customized for individual objects, providing information like what will happen if a button is clicked or describing the contents displayed within an object. Another way of using optical clues is to change the cursor symbol. For example, the standard cursor pointer could be converted to a hand or magnifying glass when it is dragged over objects that can be used to navigate to new documents in the application. Once the cursor is no longer over the object, the status line text will return to the standard text, and the cursor will change back to the standard pointer.

5.4.3.1.3 Styleguide/Development Guide

Corporate Styleguide

A corporate-wide Styleguide for information system application documents, especially one developed by or jointly with the marketing or promotional department, goes a long way towards helping information system applications become successful. For one thing, it gives all the components of the information system (or information systems) the same appearance, making them easier to use and increasing the likelihood of user acceptance. Another benefit is that, by directly involving the "creative" and "artistic" departments, tiresome arguments about identifying the "right" layout can be avoided. Without a Styleguide, system development can get bogged down (sometimes for days) by insignificant issues like deciding on which font to use. A Styleguide eliminates delays caused by minor formatting issues, and enables developers to move on to more important structural issues.

Functional Elements

The development guide displays an expanded selection of Styleguides, including functional elements along with the optical elements. The development guide is subject to constant expansion and modification. The next four chapters examine typical theme areas for a traditional development guide.

5.4.3.1.4 Sorts

Column titles with white font on a dark green background identify columns that can be used to sort display data. The sort is executed by clicking on the column title. After a sort has been executed, the sorted-by column heading will have a blue (for descending) or red (for ascending) font on a light green background. The direction of the sort changes every time the column title is clicked (i.e. if you click on a column title to do an ascending sort, the next time you click on that column title a descending sort will be executed).

Company	Price	Empoyees	Town
BASF	43,72	158.000	Ludwigshafen
Bayer	55,34	146.000	Leverkusen
Henkel	32,44	16.000	Düsseldorf
Hoechst	53,84	142.000	Frankfurt
Schering	47,23	40.000	Berlin
Veba	45,32	120.000	Gelsenkirchen

Exhibit 22: "Sorting" Styleguide Element (Ascending by Firm)

Company	Price	Empoyees	Town
BASF	43,72	158.000	Ludwigshafen
Bayer	55,34	146.000	Leverkusen
Veba	45,32	120.000	Gelsenkirchen
Hoechst	53,84	142.000	Frankfurt
Henkel	32,44	16.000	Düsseldorf
Schering	47,23	40.000	Berlin

Exhibit 23: "Sorting" Styleguide Elemen (Descending by Location)

Very Intuitive

Although this technique sounds complicated, it has proven to be very popular. It is easy to learn and use, and it has no effect on the data in the database (all sorts are local actions executed on locally-stored data). Because the action is local, sorts generally take no more than a few seconds. Inexperienced computer users are particularly fond of the sort function, because it is easy to execute and easy to follow the results.

5.4.3.1.5 Indexing

When dealing with timelines, it is possible to set the displayed values on an indexed 100% scale. The single point in time that is to serve as the 100% index value can be arbitrarily chosen by the user. This type of analysis is useful for analyzing the relative movement of displayed values.

Flexible Reference Point

Through the use of the "Index" development guide element, the index time value can be selected by simply clicking on a point on the time axis. The time axis fields have a white font on a dark green background, except for the active field which is

119

displayed in blue font on a light green background. All the values above the selected point in time will automatically set to 100. This point becomes the default comparison line. This intersection point can be moved to any other point in time, by clicking on a different point on the time axis. Like the process of defining a Sort (described earlier), this command is executed very quickly.

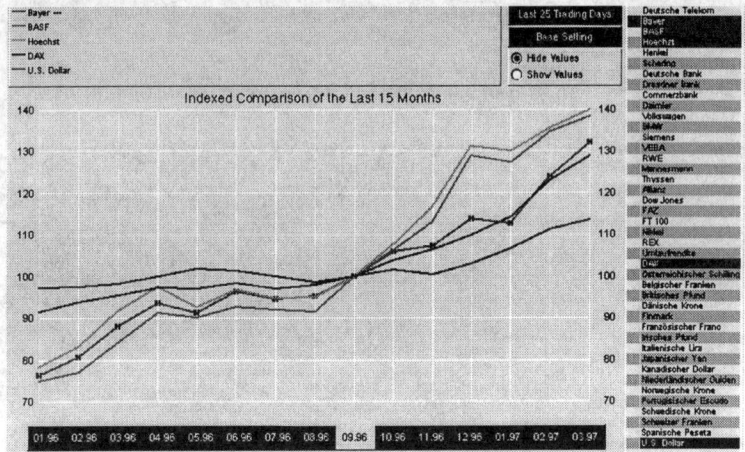

Exhibit 24: Index Styleguide Element

5.4.3.1.6   Color Scheme

The color scheme is an important part of an information system. Critical or noteworthy data can be identified with bold, striking colors. The example used here is an appointment planner, with a two color format (as dictated by the Styleguide). This list replaced a paper version of the planner that had to be typed on a typewriter. The typed list included a marking system for identifying appointments that had been changed or rescheduled. One of the requirements for the electronic appointment planner was to include a similar marking feature.

Displaying Changed
Appointments

The appointment list is stored on a central server, in a table that includes additional Yes/No columns linked to whether or not the date, time, location or discussion subject has been changed. One of inSight®'s many features is the ability to color highlight individual cells (as well as the font color and the background color) even in the context of a standardized two color format. The system developers were able to create a document that highlighted changed appointments, based on information from the server database table. In this example, changed appointments are shown with a white font color on a dark red background. A user request to display a list of all changed appointment data at the click of a button was also easily integrated into the application.

Day		Time	Meeting Title
26.3.97	We	15:00	Information Leitenc
14.4.97	Mo	08:30	Planungskonferen:
14.4.97	Mo	14:30	Information Leitenc
15.4.97	Tu	08:30	Vorstandssitzung
15.4.97	Tu	15:00	Werkskonferenz E
16.4.97	We	09:00	Werksleiterkonfere
17.4.97	Th	15:00	Information Leitenc
17.4.97	Th	15:30	Information Leitenc
21.4.97	Mo	08:30	Planungskonferen:
21.4.97	Mo	09:00	Werkskonferenz E
22.4.97	Tu	08:30	Vorstandssitzung

Exhibit 25: Color Highlighting Styleguide Element

5.4.3.1.7   "Thermometer Graph"

The "thermometer graph" is useful for tracking daily figures (like turnover) over the course of a month. This Styleguide element is not designed using a standard inSight® graph feature, but is created through the overlapping of three distinct graphs.

Recognizing Important Information at a Glance

The following example shows accounting results for individual organizational units. The gray columns display budget figures, while the blue columns display previous year figures. The application user can quickly and easily recognize whether or not the budget figures are at, above or below the previous year actual results. The red and white columns "grow" on a daily basis. They display cumulated figures for all the data up to the current date. The red columns display the cumulated actual values to date, while the white columns display the pro-rated budget totals for the current date. If the red column is higher than the red column, that particular organizational unit is ahead of the budgeted plan.

Complex Logic

In this special example, the system is also required to incorporate sales from so-called "overlap days" (those revenues that are reported after the monthly closing date). The actual display of this complicated logic is quite impressive, and was made possible by the extreme flexibility of inSight®.

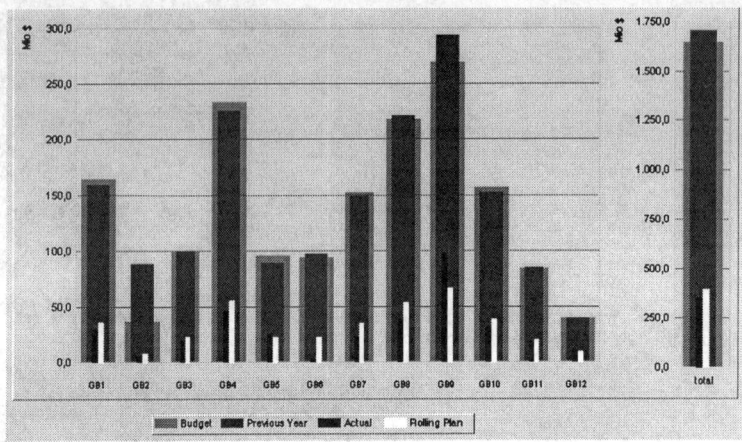

Exhibit 26: "Thermometer Graph" Styleguide Element

5.4.3.2 Development Elements

5.4.3.2.1 Dependent Menus

The contents of a dependent menu cell are driven by the available data selection. To achieve this result, it is sometimes necessary to process extremely large numbers of data records. This effort is outweighed, however, by the resulting ease of maintaining and updating system applications.

Only Existing Combinations can be Chosen

A particularly attractive feature of the program is the ability to only display those contents for which the database table has values. For example, a menu object will only display those countries for which the data table has sales figures.

Dependent menu cells make it easier to navigate within the application, and greatly reduce the amount of data that needs to be transferred to the application. If the user selects a region like "Europe," only European countries will appear in the display. If the user then selects an individual land, the next menu object will only display those products sold in that land.

If variable dependencies are used with two menu objects, only those menu selection combinations will appear for which a value is stored in the database. An "empty" response will never appear on the end user's screen (it is important to note the distinction between "zero," where the actual value "0" is displayed, and "empty," where no display appears).

An example: The turnover figures for a corporation can be broken down by the subsidiary that registered the sales or by the business unit responsible for the sales. The user can also select to see turnover figures for a "business unit within a subsidiary." Of course, not all combinations of business units and subsidiaries will have data records. In the actual turnover display for the entire corporation, the menus will show all the business units and subsidiaries that have registered turnover results. If the selected business unit is changed, the subsidiary will change so that only those subsidiaries with sales for the selected business unit appear. If the subsidiary menu selection is changed, the same process will occur for the business unit menu. Regardless of what selection changes are made in the business unit or subsidiary menus, the selection in the month menu will remain unchanged.

As is so often the case, the tricky aspects involved with this technology are difficult to describe. The idea of working with menu contents with changing dependency relationships has evolved into one of the most popular application design concepts. The menu dependency displayed below was very easy to define.

Easy to Create
Variable
Dependencies

The selected business unit GB4 only has operations in the displayed countries. On a related note, only the BUs operating in Canada are displayed in the business unit menu. The reciprocal menu dependency technology insures that no combinations can be selected for which there is no data. By selecting "All BUs," the user will see the complete list of countries in the countries menu. By selecting "All Countries," the user will see the complete list of BUs in the BU menu.

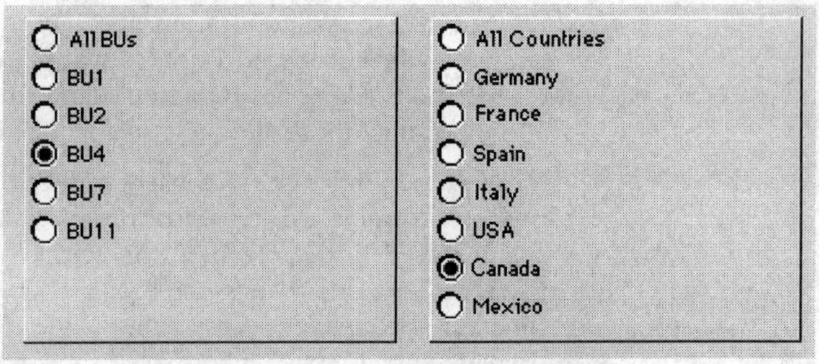

○ All BUs	○ All Countries
○ BU1	○ Germany
○ BU2	○ France
◉ BU4	○ Spain
○ BU7	○ Italy
○ BU11	○ USA
	◉ Canada
	○ Mexico

Exhibit 27: Dependent Menu Styleguide Element

5.4.3.2.2   ## Visible/Invisible

An inSight® application consists of multiple inSight® documents, on which objects are displayed (see page 55). Different functions can be linked to these objects (i.e. clicking on an object opens an existing inSight® document), making it possible to create and maintain related applications.

Compact Application Possibilities

Since every inSight® document corresponds to a physical PC file, it makes sense to use as few documents as is possible. The function PROPERTIES was designed to help developers achieve this goal. Individual objects can be temporarily defined as "visible" or "invisible", making it possible to switch entire objects group on or off of a single document. Developers can thus use a single document to display multiple data perspectives.

5.4.3.2.3   ## Program Loops

When developing applications with inSight®, program loops are not an important development technique. In most cases, they are not needed. However, there are certain instances where problems can only be solved with the help of a programming loop.

Using Tables From Different Database Systems

This example outlines a technique that a developer can use to combine tables from different databases. A developer has a locally-stored table containing an "employee ID number" column. The developer wants to pull back (on a periodic basis) employee information like name, department, and telephone number from a central database table. To do this, inSight® uses a trick: A menu cell with employee ID numbers from the central table data is switched to "individual selection," and then the employee ID number from the local database is copied into the menu cell. The central table sends back detailed employee information based on the menu cell selection. This function can only be used if the menu cell contains no more than 29 values. With 30 or more values, an error message will appear.

This problem can be avoided using a program loop: The developer just needs to copy different blocks (with up to 29 values) into the menu cell.

5.4.3.2.4   Naming Conventions

The vast possibilities for creating display documents within an information system make it essential to develop a simple and effective document naming convention. This is especially true when working with a Windows 3.1x version, where file names are limited to eight characters. It makes little sense to use common terms or everyday phrases, as they are easily misinterpreted. A simple and effective solution is a key code system. The following is an example of an eight character key code system:

aabbccdd.isd

The codes represent:

aa	alphanumeric abbreviation for the specific information system
bb	alphanumeric code for the specific topic
cc	alphanumeric code for the specific subject
dd	sequential numeric code for the specific document
.isd	Windows operating system extension

Example: The file "UI020301.isd" belongs to the corporate-wide information system (UI), under the topic 02 (Market/Exchange) with the subject 03 (Before Hours/After Hours Market). As a further identifier, the file deals with page 01 of the subject.

5.4.3.3   Examples

5.4.3.3.1   Start-Up Sheet

Current Information, Communication

The design of a corporate-wide start-up sheet can quickly develop into a delicate political issue. While some users will prefer a less crowded, optically appealing start-up sheet, others will push for a more sober appearance with as many information access links as possible. Another concept is to design the start-up sheet so that, in addition to providing access links to important business or subject areas, it also automatically provides a display of the most current and important corporate information tidbits. This requires that the start-up sheet be updated on a regular basis. The best way to do this is to use a counter on the PC application for checking the currently-displayed information against the most recent information loaded on the server. When new information is loaded on to the server, the counter on the server will not match the counter on the PC, causing the application to automatically load over the newest data. The counter on the PC is also updated, so the whole process can begin anew when the server is once again loaded with newer data.

Important corporate information includes breaking news stories, financial market information, currency exchange rates, and stories about major and minor competitors. This start-up sheet design, which is really the first step in creating an electronic newspaper, generally meets with high user acceptance. Such a design realizes the goal of having the user switch the system on first thing in the morning, and not switching the system off until the workday has ended. If use of the system becomes pervasive, it is easier for an MIS to establish itself as a critical corporate resource.

Signal Buttons

It makes sense to prominently display the theme areas, with up to six themes per area (see below), on the user start-up sheet. As an extra feature, a signaling system can be used to identify themes with new or changed information. A common method is to change the button color from green to red if new information is available. Once the user has accessed the new information, the button will return to its original green color. The user is able to determine which theme areas should use the signaling system. The data necessary for the button color coding is stored and administered in a central table.

Communication functions and modifiable buttons should be used to supplement the start-up sheet. Modifiable buttons can be further classified into those with user-dependent functions and those with PC-dependent functions. User-dependent settings should be centrally-stored, so that users will encounter the same settings regardless of which computer they use to access the system. PC-dependent settings, on the other hand, should be stored locally on the PC. These settings are unique to the configuration of the given PC, and are useless on any other PC. Centrally administering all the PCs within a company would require too much time and effort.

A start-up sheet could be designed as follows:

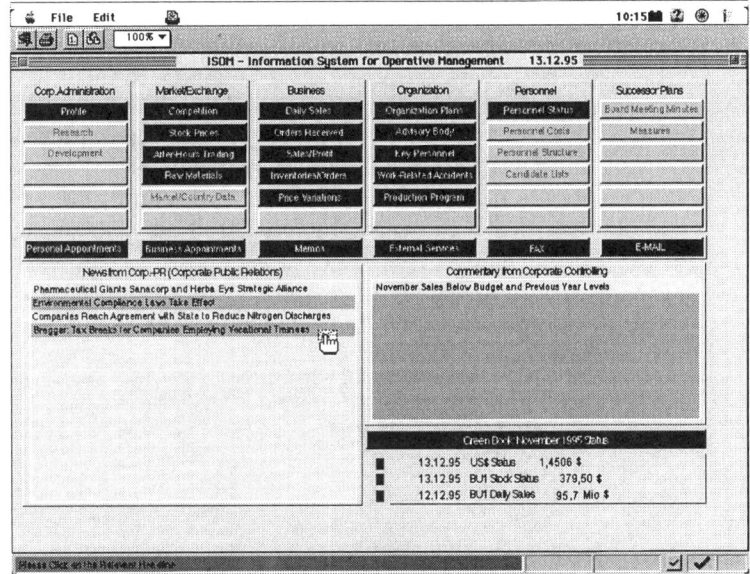

Exhibit 28: Application Start-Up Sheet

Planned application themes are identified by green buttons.

An example of a PC-dependent function is calling up a day planner program on the PC. The information needed to launch the program, like file names and paths, is stored in a local file on the PC. These files can be maintained and updated as necessary by individual users, or by an employee from the data processing department.

When starting an application, the user does not launch the actual start-up sheet. Instead, an administrative document checks to see how current the user's start-up sheet is, and replaces it with a more current version if one is available (see page 178).

As part of the system's access permission design (see page 146) users will encounter light green buttons that identify areas of the system to which they are not granted access privileges. The biggest downside to this solution are the employee morale issues that may arise from users being directly confronted with their "low" status within the system (i.e. within the company). However, experience has shown that this design is better than simply presenting users with an almost empty start-up screen.

5.4.3.3.2

Sales/Profit Display

Information related to sales and profit data can be displayed on a single (with the help of the visible/invisible option, see page 54) or several different inSight® documents. The initial display traces the development of sales and profits over a period of time (usually twelve months), for budget, actual, and previous year results. The user can choose to display "monthly" data or "cumulated" data (the sum of all the data since the start of the current year).

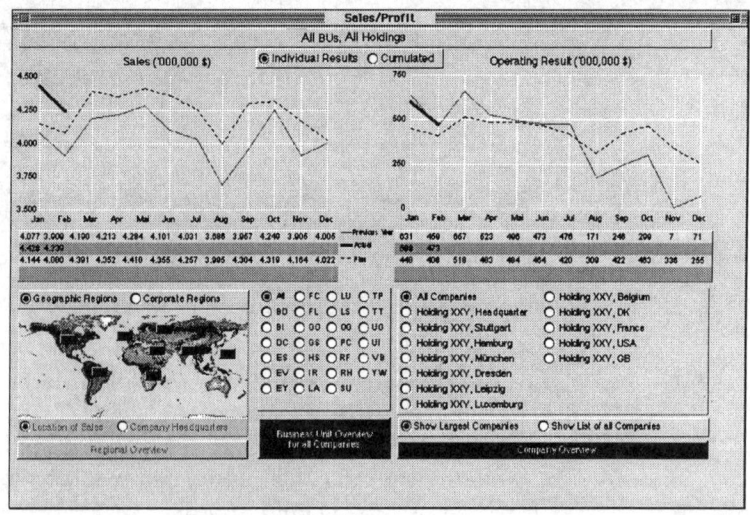

Exhibit 29: Sales/Profits Display

The selection objects below the graphic display enable the user to view data based on regional, organizational, and subsidiary structures. For regional displays, the user can choose between "geographic regions" and "corporate regions." With regards to overall corporate results, consolidated data from any of the twelve largest subsidiaries can be selected. It is also possible to view a list of all subsidiaries (over 300 of them); if a single subsidiary is selected, its consolidated data is then displayed.

Selection of Subsidiaries with the Highest Turnover

The three navigation radio buttons are all related to each other based on the data in the data source (see page 122). When a specific organization unit is selected, only subsidiaries related to that unit will appear in the subsidiary selection: The twelve subsidiaries with the highest turnover results will appear in the subsidiary radio button. When a specific subsidiary is selected, only organizational areas that have turnover or profit results for that subsidiary will appear. The "All" selection in the organization units menu (as well as the "All Subsidiaries" menu selection) can be used to return the document display to the figures for the entire respective category selections.

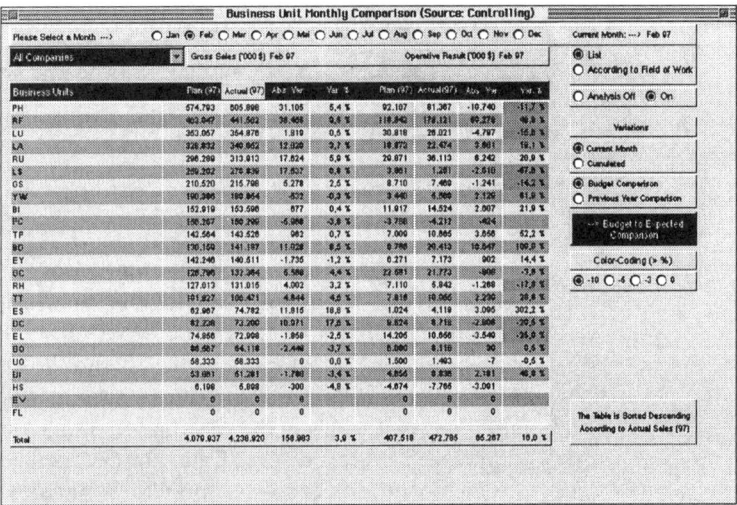

Exhibit 30: Sales/Profit Display List

So that employees in a given department can quickly access the data that is relevant to their work, a user-dependent navigation mechanism (and centrally-linked menu cell selections) was designed. This saves inexperienced or hurried users the aggravation of hunting for necessary documents or attribute combinations within a document.

The "Overview of All Business Units" button on the bottom part of the screen opens a document listing detailed information about all business units for a given month.

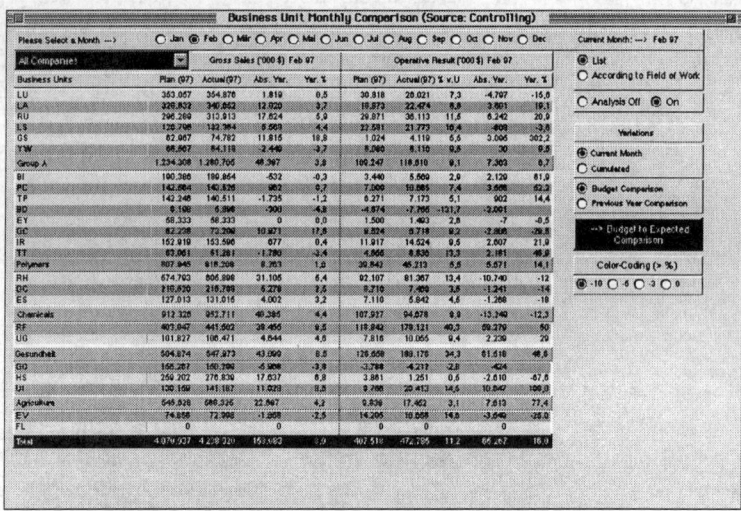

Exhibit 31: Sales/Profit Display by Business Unit

Analysis Button

With the help of an "analysis button," actual monthly data can be compared to budget or previous year data for an individual subsidiary, or for the cumulated total of all subsidiaries. The list can be sorted according to the Styleguide guidelines (see page 118). Particularly large variations are color-coded. The user is able to set the acceptable variation range using the corresponding radio button object. Data can be displayed in a list form, or it can be modified so the individual business units are grouped together based on the organizational reporting structure (via the radio button in the upper right-hand corners of Exhibits 30 and 31).

The sales/profits area of the application also contains seven further display possibilities, including a document displaying detailed information for individual subsidiaries, and a document displaying country totals data based on the headquarters of customers.

5.4.3.3.3   Organization Plan

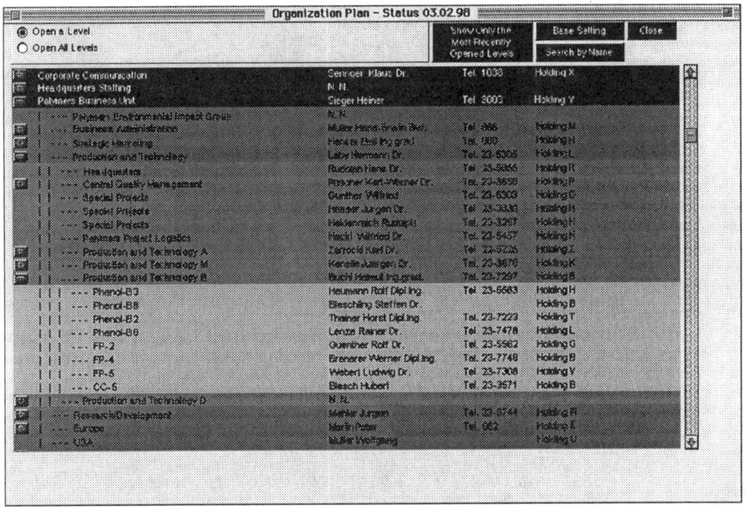

Exhibit 32: Hierarchical Organization Plan

Organization plans have traditionally been drawn using a pyramid diagram. With corporate organization structures becoming flatter and flatter, it is not uncommon to have ten or more employees on the same hierarchical level and reporting to the same person. The pyramid diagram is not suited to displaying this type of structure. As a result, the organization plan is now often displayed in the form of a list, from which one is able to "drill down" to the list of subordinates.

A second display for this data can be used to search for employees by name.

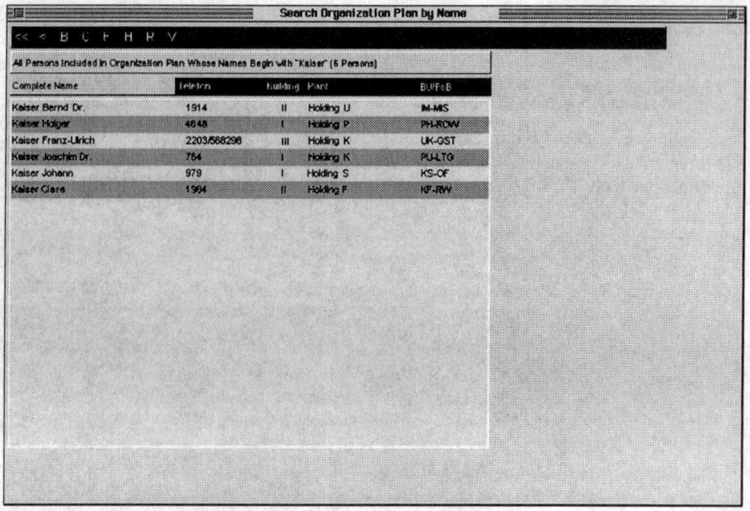

Search Organization Plan by Name			
<< < B C F H K V			
All Persons Included in Organization Plan Whose Names Begin with "Kaiser" (6 Persons)			
Complete Name	Telefon	Holding Part	BUFcB
Kaiser Bernd Dr.	1914	II Holding U	M-MS
Kaiser Holger	4648	I Holding P	PH-ROW
Kaiser Franz-Ulrich	2203/588298	III Holding K	UK-GST
Kaiser Joachim Dr.	784	I Holding K	PU-LTG
Kaiser Johann	979	I Holding S	KS-OF
Kaiser Clara	1964	II Holding F	KF-RW

Exhibit 33: Organization Plan; Search by Name

Key Personnel

Another form for an organization plan is to list the managing director and supervisory board of the individual subsidiaries. This information would be accessed from a central display listing all the subsidiaries, organized by region and country.

It is possible to get more details about any of the people included in the list of key personnel, by simply clicking on that person's name. As an example, it might be informative to list out all the titles and functional responsibilities held by that person.

Advisory Body

Chemicals, Chicago

Holding in Subsidiary (as a %)

| | Holding XXY, Plant N.Y. | 50,0000 |

Body	Key Personnel	Title	Dele-gate to	Year of Birth	Joined Comp.	In Office Since	Election Year	Successor Year
Supervisory Board	Kramer, Manfred	Managing Director		1940	1981	1981	1986	
	Nimmer, Franz	Plant Manager		1936	1976	1990	1992	
	Febel, Reiner	Board Member	XXY	1932	1980	1986	1992	
	Heumann, Claus	Member	XXY	1944	1976	1994	1994	
	Bauth, Rudi	Member		1940		1994	1994	
	Rottcher, Wolfgang	Member		1940		1990	1992	
	Bson-Smith, Dr. Chris	Member		1940		1990	1992	
	Pals, Dr. Udo	Member	XXY	1937	1967	1988	1992	
	Anderson, Bryan K.	Substitute Member	XXY	1939	1969	1994	1994	
	Vogel, Winfried	Substitute Member		1977		1990	1992	
	Aanderlich, Dr. Hermann	Acting Board Member, ABM		1938		1989	1992	
	Schwer, Manfred	ABM		1940		1987	1992	
	Feetz, Dr. Ing. Wilfried J.	ABM		1951		1987	1992	
	Such, Dr. Siegfried	ABM		1947		1991	1992	
	Immer, Hubert-Wilhelm	ABM		1942		1992	1992	
	Delis, Hans	ABM		1946		1992	1992	
Advisory Council	Boger, Winfried	ABM Substitute Member		1940		1992	1992	
	Dimone Dr. Chris	ABM Substitute Member		1943		1992	1992	
	Sanders, Dr. Hubert	ABM Substitute Member		1937		1992	1992	
	Pfing, Manfred	ABM Substitute Member		1941		1992	1992	
	Charbon, Dr. Volker	Member		1946		1996		
	Schmsck, Hans	Member	XXY	1944	1976	1994		
	Immer, Hubert-Wilhelm	Member		1940		1990		
	Pfenk, Jurgen	Member		1940		1994		
	Aanderlich, Dr. Hermann	Member	XXY	1932	1960	1985		
	Haard, Dr. Hans	Member	XXY	1937	1987	1988		

Exhibit 34: Overview of Subsidiaries

Key Personnel

O # O A O B @ C O D O E O F O G O H O I O J O K O L O M O N O O O P O R O O O S O T O U O V O W O X O Y O Z

Charbon, Dr. Volker

Company	Country	Body	Assumed Position	Joined	Election	Successor
Holding XXY, Headquarter	Germany	Advisory Council	Managing Director	1994	1994	
Holding XXY, Plant Stuttgart	Germany	Advisory Council	Substitute Member	1994	1994	
Holding XXY, Plant Dresden	Germany		Acting Board Member	1994	1996	
Holding XXY, Plant Hamburg	Germany		Member	1994		
Holding XXY, Plant Mainz	Germany		Managing Director	1994		
Holding XXY, Plant Belgium	Belgium	Supervisory Board	Member	1994	1995	
Holding XXY, Plant Leipzig	Germany		Managing Director	1994		

Exhibit 35: Overview of Manager Responsibilities

5.4.3.3.4 Stock Market Information

The stock market information main sheet displays the current and previous day values for stocks, exchange rates, and indexes, along with related analyses (trend arrows, %-variations, absolute variations). The information can be sorted (either ascending or

133

descending) by clicking on the column title by which the data is to be sorted. If a user clicks on a specific stock, currency, or index, a new display with values from the last 18 days and the last 17 months appears. Comparisons can be made using any of the individual values from the last 15 months or last 25 trading days. As described on page 119, it is also possible to select various currencies from a list, and to set all their values at 100 for a selected point in time. This makes it possible to trace the rise and fall of the currencies relative to one another. A marker can be used (tied to a currency by clicking on an identifier next to the name of the selected currency) to optically separate one currency from the others in the display.

The point in time used in the comparison can be selected by clicking on a date on the time axis. The selected point in time will be color highlighted within the time axis.

The values of the currencies relative to each other can also be displayed.

5.4.3.3.5 Investments

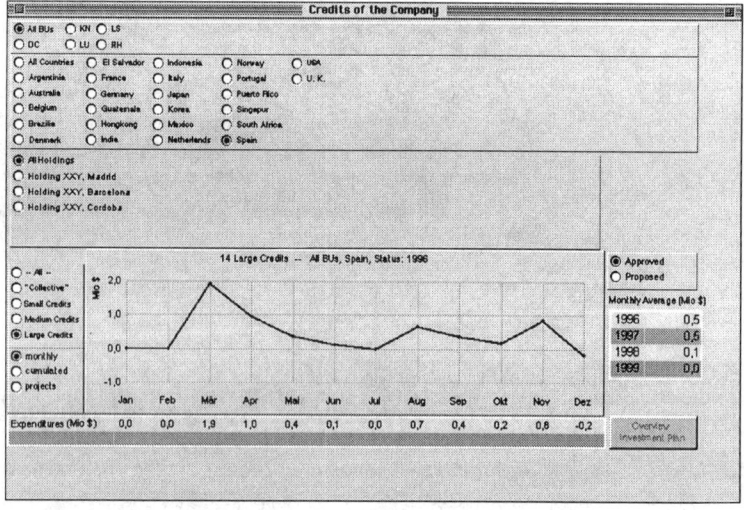

Exhibit 36: Investments

The investments theme shows monthly, cumulated, or individual project expenditures. Figures can be displayed by countries, divisions, plants, or any combinations thereof. When cumulated displays are selected, it may be helpful to include a linear projection through the end of the year. Investments can be grouped into classifications like small investments, medium investments (from $250,000 to $2,500,000) and large investments (over $2,500,000). The approved and planned investments for the coming year are displayed as full-year totals. The projects within the selected classification are sub-classified as planned and approved projects, and can be sorted according to Styleguide rules (see page 118). By clicking on an individual project, a manager can access more detailed information about that investment.

Display Combinations at all Levels

Every possible combination can be displayed at any of the available levels. The menu contents are data-driven (see page 122), so every user selection is guaranteed to be a data "hit" (i.e. only menu selection combinations for which there is data are available to the users).

5.5 Planning Content Releases

5.5.1 Acceptance

If the developer decides to list the application themes in the start-up sheet, there is an obligation to completely address these themes in the application. If the system promises to address a theme, users will expect to have quick and comprehensive access to data related to the theme. On the other hand, an information system in the early stages of development will look less than impressive if only those themes that are ready are displayed. Such a strategy makes it that much harder to garner widespread corporate acceptance and enthusiasm for the system.

Each MIS administrator is responsible for selecting one of these system variations. In a favorable development environment, namely one with the unconditional support of upper management, it is a good idea to use the full start-up sheet (i.e., to list all the active and planned themes). This makes it easier to integrate the various application themes, and reduces the risk of parallel development by other projects or departments.

Support from Upper Management

The original goal of an MIS was to completely support managers' decision-making processes with data processing-supported technical resources. But even today there is a dearth of truly easy-to-use integrated programs. As an example, there is no program capable of closing presentation displays when they are not being used, and then re-opening them when an important business partner phones. The creation of such "thinking" office applications remains a distant goal. Even electronic day planners in the shapes and sizes available today have failed to permeate the prevailing business culture. A truly integrated and easy-to-use office support application requires (among other things) a (functioning) language recognition feature, which the software industry has been promising for the last 15 years. Even if this problem is solved, a program that can capture and model the complexities of the modern business world remains a moving target. Managers and executives would need to completely re-design their working habits to take advantage of such technology. To date, only a few managers have shown an openness and willingness to take this step.

It is no wonder then, that the only really successful and accepted functional elements of information system programs are those that simply display already-processed data. The most popular application themes have been those that are oriented towards the particular demands of leadership positions. An application with six theme areas, each containing six separate themes, presents the user with a total of 36 possible information analyses. It is not recommended that a start-up sheet offer the user more choices than this.

More information related to these subjects can be found starting on page 81.

5.5.2   Timeline

Information Quality

The establishment of a timeline for the introduction of application themes is dependent on the quality of the information delivered to the system. When dealing with data that is periodically updated, the people responsible for the system need to insure that the raw data is delivered consistently according to a fixed schedule, and that it is always high quality data (i.e. accurate and complete). Once again, practical experience has proven that few existing data repository systems are capable of completely fulfilling these requirements. Most need to be modified, adjusted or in extreme cases completely rebuilt. Depending on the situation, this process can last up to several years. Responsibility for this work should remain in the department or division that was responsible for the data content even before the information system concept was developed. The path of least resistance for the process of implementing the information system is the creation of a complete information processing chain (described in more detail on page 166 ff). It has also been found that support and encouragement from the information system team has positive repercussions for the long-term success of the system.

When building a system, the theme areas with the most confidential information and the largest amount of text entries present the biggest challenges. Software companies have yet to develop a method for loading already-encoded data on to a data server, making it more difficult to protect highly sensitive information (like personal data related to high-level corporate executives). Such an encoding system would insure that even the employees responsible for maintaining the system would not be able to read the data. To decode the data, a user needs a special card that is recognized by a reading device attached to a PC. The data encryption technologies available today have not yet developed a system capable of meeting these security needs.

Formatted Texts

As far as formatted texts are concerned, it is difficult to access these texts for the system using traditional relational database technology. This functional shortcoming is a major problem with SAP®-EIS. inSight®, in conjunction with relational databases, offers a clever solution. It is able to take formatted information and cut it into ASCII character strings, and then save these strings (in the form of data records) to a database table. When the information is needed in a display screen, the object is reassembled and displayed in an object window. Using these functions available only in inSight®, formatted texts, OLE objects and even entire files can be stored to a database. Logically, inSight® is not able to display a complete file in its interface; it can however, cause the file to be written back to a hard drive or portable drive. To use a concrete example, OLE technology has been used to take hundreds of strategy portfolios developed in MS Excel®and display them directly in the information system, without actually installing MS Excel® on the end user PCs.

HTML as a "Quasi" Standard

With the explosion in popularity of the Internet, the HTML language is developing into more and more of a "Quasi" standard for unstructured information. It is easy to construct and prepare unstructured information using a web server, and browser technology makes it easy to display the contents. To keep pace with

137

this technology, inSight® (starting with version 2.0) includes a browser object directly in the program, which can be used to display HTML objects. The HTML page address (URL) can be input as a parameter directly from a database (see also page 101). inSight® programmers are currently working on an encryption concept that will send HTML data in an unreadable form across the network. After the user's access privileges have been checked (access rights are stored in the database as well), the information is decoded directly on the user's PC, without forcing the user to enter an additional password. This process, which has correctly been compared to Pay-TV, serves as the basis for charging users who access information stored in the corporate Intranet for specific user groups ("PayNet?").

5.5.3   Information Levels

There are many reasons why an information system should not provide access to all the data that is technically accessible. First, all the corporate data must be processed so that it can be properly interpreted, regardless of the user's familiarity with the data. A bigger problem occurs when managers have questions about information from the lowest data levels. These questions can not be "electronically answered." They demand research (often extensive) from other departments and corporate entities. But when managers have been surveyed, the results have uniformly indicated that access to detailed levels of corporate data is absolutely unnecessary for their decision making processes. The problem is when access to these lower levels of data is granted, managers look at this data and develop questions related to it. In many cases, the questions are related to variations that are not directly related to business conditions, but rather stem from base data processing or technical system issues.

Traffic Light Function

Even the popular "traffic light function" designed to alert the end user to significant data variations, is not fool-proof. The following example illustrates how data from the lowest data level can be misinterpreted when a traffic light display is used.

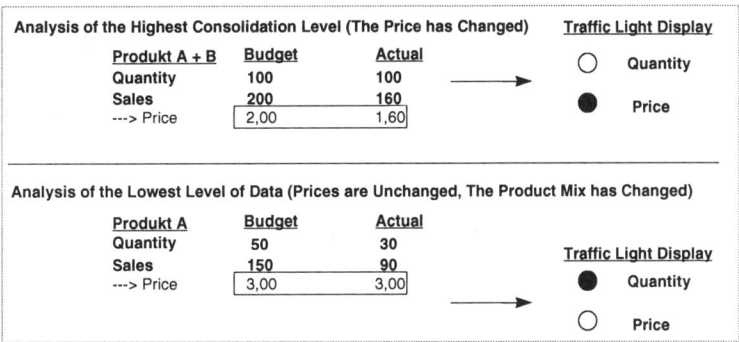

Exhibit 37: Traffic Light Logic

The use of functions like the traffic light graph only makes sense when more detailed levels of data are available. Otherwise, the mathematical data may be misinterpreted. In this case, the user will not realize that the apparent price variation is due to missed sales targets, not actual price fluctuations. Less of the more expensive product was sold, while the company was able to move more of the cheaper product. At the higher, more summarized data level, it is impossible to identify this change in the product sales mix.

The case for subdividing data is particularly convincing when dealing with a large data repository with multiple hierarchical levels. Taking a monthly business results report as an example, the various hierarchical levels of the report were defined as strata within a pyramid structure (see graph page 15). The information level is found in the middle of the pyramid. This is the lowest data level that an information system user is able to access. The two data levels below the information level can be used in mathematical analyses by the employees responsible for calculating and interpreting these results in the overall corporate context.

Information Level,
Research Level

The following definitions and basic principles can be formulated for the information levels in a data pyramid:

- The **Information Level** is the lowest consolidated level which is included in information system reporting.
- The **Research Level** is the lowest mechanically-calculated consolidated level of information.
- **Basic Principle 1**: The information level must, and the research level should, contain controlled and confirmed data.

- **Basic Principle 2**: If the research level is two levels below the information level in an information system, questions from the information level can be answered quickly and relatively inexpensively.
- **Basic Principle 3**: Moving from the information level to lower consolidation levels , even if it is technically possible, can have a negative impact on the speed and cost with which research level analyses are executed.

Separate Research
Modules

It is therefore recommended that a company work with research modules in addition to information systems. Analysts and controllers should have access to all corporate data for their work with these research modules. A research module can be much simpler in design than an information system, as the emphasis is on function over form.

5.6   Planning the System Roll-Out

Strategy plays an important role in the roll-out of a comprehensive corporate information system. The best scenario involves using board members as the first wave of end users. An implementation that begins "at the top" lends a sense of credibility and prestige to the system. It is often helpful to integrate the board members' secretaries into the initial roll-out as well. On the one hand, directly involving the secretaries in an important project will appeal to their sense of pride, and likely generate a degree of loyalty to the system. On the other hand, the secretaries can act as the "first resort" when the board members have questions or problems with the system. Further, the secretaries can act as a feedback conduit, relaying problems and complaints to the system administrators before the board members grow frustrated with the system.

Integrating the
Secretaries

It is essential for the system administrators to build up a sense of trust between the board members and themselves (see page 168). A good tactic for successfully creating trust and confidence is to offer board members personal consulting and training when they are first introduced to PCs (or the information system itself).

Roll-Out from Top to
Bottom

Later roll-out phases should proceed hierarchically down the corporate chain of command. For example, the second wave of system users might include divisional vice-presidents, while the third wave would provide senior managers access to the system. Parallel to granting these executives access to the system, the system administrators should be sure that key employees who work for these executives also have some degree of access to the data (for more information about "access classes," see page 180).

Corporate-Wide Access

The final roll-out should provide access to the system for all the divisions and departments within the corporation. Of course, their access to the system should be limited to those applications and documents that are relevant to their corporate functions.

An almost more important goal for the development of an information system is the selection and testing of appropriate hardware and software. Most companies lack a data processing system that completely fulfills the requirements of an "information system." Some companies embellish their base operative systems with the title "information system," but one rarely encounters a manager within these companies who is willing and able to retrieve strategic information from these systems. Even marketing information systems, so frequently discussed and praised, are limited to displaying information in list form.

Data Processing Infrastructure

One of the obligations associated with developing a corporate-wide information system is the use of technology that is compatible with the overall corporate data processing infrastructure. The technology chosen should also be flexible enough to be used for similar projects in other areas of the corporation. From the very beginning, it is important to consider the unique interests of application developers and information managers as well as end users:

Requirements from the Users' Perspective:

- Easy-to-Use
- Overall System Clarity
- Availability of Analysis Methods
- Graphic Display Possibilities
- Complements and Exploits Existing Applications
- Fast Response Times
- Protection of Private Data

Requirements from the Developers' Perspective:

- High-Performance Developer Tools
- Abundance of Generator Functions

141

- Easy to Adjust the Data Structure
- Easy to Change / Modify Application Documents
- Easy Administration of the MIS Data
- Easy Integration into the Existing Infrastructure

Requirements from the Information Managers' Perspective:

- Conformance to Standards
- Support of the Architecture Strategy
- Flexible Expansion Possibilities
- High Quality Vendor Service
- Complete Support

Few Appropriate
Software Solutions

Most of the larger software houses develop their software in compliance with the traditional needs of information managers and developers. As a result, the interface programs they sell are complex and not suited for use by managers. The programs are very similar to transaction systems, whose requirements (in terms of an interface) are very different from those of a high-level MIS: The employees who use a transaction system receive comprehensive training on the system. It should be noted that these employees spend a number of hours every day working with the system, so that they are well-versed in all its subtleties and nuances. However, it should also be noted that these employees are literally forced to learn how to operate the transaction system, because that is what they are paid to do. There is no comparable pressure forcing a manager to use an information system. If a manager is unsatisfied with the information system, or finds it to be too complicated, there are a number of alternative methods for gathering needed information. The easiest solution is to delegate the responsibility for information gathering to a subordinate. The costs to the corporation for this time expenditure are not included in the central "information gathering" costs total. Thus, there is often a relatively large disparity in the costs comparison between a data processing-supported information system (whose costs are readily apparent) and the more traditional "information gathering" process (whose costs are often obscure or hidden).

Even the array of powerful MIS software packages designed by smaller firms fall short when it comes to developing an easy-to-use interface for the transaction systems mentioned above. Some of the features and functions in these software packages offer amazing development and design possibilities; unfortunately, these features and functions can only be fully exploited by experienced and trained users. Employees without a technical background and employees who have not been trained to use the software have no idea how to properly use the majority of the functions available. The problem is, these employees are exactly the users who need to work directly with the data on their own PCs.

SAP-GUI Targets Limited User Segments

SAP®-EIS with the SAP proprietary user interface (SAP-GUI) does not meet the needs and expectations of PC-inexperienced end users. The SAP-GUI was designed for technically savvy controllers and assistants. This is illustrated by the fact that the program includes a feature for transferring data into MS Word® and MS Excel® files. When one considers the target group of a corporate-wide information system, the SAP-GUI is not the best choice.

inSight® Predecessors

From a technical perspective, one of the most important considerations for an information system is the development of an attractive user interface that is "fun" to use. It helps if users are proud of the system, and eager to show it off to others. In one documented effort to achieve this goal, a prototype interface program by the name of macControl II (see page 187) was jointly developed with a small, innovative Düsseldorf-based software firm. MacControl II was capable of directly access data from central SQL databases using SQL queries that were automatically generated by the program. This impressive program enjoyed great success and popularity among the board members who used it for over two years. However, because the program was only designed for the APPLE Macintosh platform, it was not able to gain widespread acceptance within the company or among consumers in general. The heir to macControl II's throne appears to be inSight®, which, in addition to offering expanded and improved features and functions, was developed on the Windows-NT platform. One of the most impressive added features in inSight® is the ability to directly access data in SAP®-EIS reports. Since inSight® was basically developed by the same programming team that created macControl, it is not surprising that the program is also compatible with the APPLE Macintosh platform. This made it possible for older applications to be ported over to inSight® without any major complications or difficulties.

<table>
<tr><td>Information
"Marketing"</td><td>The rules for building an information system are the same regardless of whether the data is stored in SAP®-EIS or in relational databases. As important as the data supply mechanisms are, care should also be taken to insure that they consist of simple and easy-to-follow processes. But even the best data supply system does not guarantee a good information system. Creating a data processing-driven information "marketing" plan is a formidable challenge, one for which very few experts with practical experience exist. This is true not only for corporate-internal employees, but also for the majority of consultants and consulting firms.</td></tr>
</table>

Information "Marketing"

The rules for building an information system are the same regardless of whether the data is stored in SAP®-EIS or in relational databases. As important as the data supply mechanisms are, care should also be taken to insure that they consist of simple and easy-to-follow processes. But even the best data supply system does not guarantee a good information system. Creating a data processing-driven information "marketing" plan is a formidable challenge, one for which very few experts with practical experience exist. This is true not only for corporate-internal employees, but also for the majority of consultants and consulting firms.

If a company decides to exploit the experiences and mental capital gained from instituting an information system, it needs to decide upon a tactic for transferring internal "know how." This can be done through training classes, seminars and an application develop hotline service. Regardless of the knowledge transfer method that is decided upon, it should always include provisions for certain MIS hot spots like database technology, SAP programs, networks, servers, PCs and the inSight® application program. Knowledge related to information system content is also an important corporate resource. It doesn't matter how good a corporation's technological abilities are if it is unable to provide users with the data displays that they need to make important strategic and operative decisions.

Developer Lessons

One quickly realizes that the success of future MIS applications, along with the widespread integration of new technologies, is reliant on the transfer of skills and knowledge from developer to developer. There are few corporations that have gone so far as to establish protocols for insuring that knowledge is shared across diverse information system projects. What is becoming very clear is that the standard procedures used to successfully develop transaction systems are not transferable to information system development (see page 75).

Modular Development

Even in the initial conceptual phases of building an information system, it is important to design the overall system along the lines of a modular structure. In principle, each individual system theme area should be able to exist as a stand-alone system. The start-up page merely serves as an "organizer" that displays and links the various thematic modules available to end users. As a logical consequence of this, it is then possible to use the individual "business objects" in different corporate information system. The start-up page for the various systems will be different, but the modules that run behind them can be the same from one system to the next. The modular concept also applies to SAP®-EIS, whereby each SAP®-EIS aspect corresponds to a theme area.

The modular concept pushes the importance of an MIS "system idea" to the background. In its place, theme-oriented business objects take center stage. Business objects can be grouped together according to user needs and the various information landscapes within a corporation. Behind each module stands a publisher/producer. As an example, the marketing department may be responsible for maintaining and administering the competitor analysis theme area. The publisher/producer is responsible for insuring that the information displayed is timely and correct, and for administering user access privileges. The emphasis changes to building systems from combinations of existing modules, instead of building a complete system from scratch.

Information as a Product

The publisher should be allowed to charge those users who access his/her module. The costs should be reasonable, as they are only meant to cover the expenses associated with gathering, processing and displaying the information. The information is thus converted to a product; in order to remain a viable component of a corporate information system, the product must be constantly adapted and modified to meet the changing needs and desires of consumers (the end users). If the module is unable to find enough acceptance (i.e. if the costs of the module exceed the revenues it generates), the module will likely be removed from the system.

Ability to Implement a "Pay-Per-Use" Policy

There are very few corporations that have embraced the "pay-per-use" form for information system transactions. Perhaps this is due to the fact that most corporate information systems are in the early stages of development, and the cost-intensive nature of the start-up phase would discourage users from accessing such expensive information. On the other hand, intense pressure like this could have a positive effect on the overall quality of the modules, and lead to a more conscious effort to improve the total value of the information system. However a company decides to proceed, it should build up the information system (and other related applications) in such a way that it is possible to at some point institute a "pay-per-use."

5.7   Help Programs

5.7.1   Individual User Settings

5.7.1.1   The Difference Between User- and PC-Specific Information

Individual settings play a pivotal role in increasing the comfort (and thereby the acceptance) of an MIS. At this point in time, it is important to draw a distinction between user- and PC-specific settings.

Unlike PC-specific settings (see page 128), which are only valid for individual PCs, user-specific settings can be centrally-stored and administered, meaning that an individual user can access his or her personal settings from any PC. The following examples stem from real-life information system implementation experiences.

5.7.1.2   Access Classes

Access classes make it easier to administer user rights within a system. This strategy is usually effective, as system users can be grouped into classes based on their different information needs and their position within the firm. Based on the access class of a user, certain system themes will not be available. If they click on a button that would normally take them to a prohibited theme, the button will not execute the function defined in it. The color of the "off-limit" button will change from green to light green. Data protection should also be practiced at the database level, so unauthorized users are unable to access confidential data via other query tools.

Four Access Classes   In a corporate-wide information system, four access classes are usually enough to meet data security requirements. The "official" system users are grouped into class 1. Every user in class 1 has full access to all the information in the system.

Class 2 users can not access important strategic data. Class 3 users are also locked out of strategic data, but also data related to personnel issues and important operative data (like sales and profits). Class 4 users can only view publicly-released data, like stock prices, currency exchange rates, accident statistics, etc.

Class 2 and 3 designations are generally given to all the assistants, controllers and other employees who work for class 1 managers. All other employees can be given class 4 access privileges. System architects should welcome these designations, as they can only expand overall corporate exposure to the system, thereby contributing to internal system acceptance. Also, important experience can be gained in terms of optimizing system performance when system usage is heavy.

Class D for Developers

System developers are granted class D privileges, which allows them to access modules that are still under development. Applications automatically start in developer mode for class D users. The developer mode, in contrast to the user mode, includes a functional tool window which is helpful in the application development process.

5.7.1.3   News

The handling of "news" is one of the most interesting issues related to developing an information system. New information can automatically appear on the users' screens, or signals can be built into the application alerting users to the arrival of new information. If new (i.e. updated) information related to a particular application theme becomes available, this can be indicated by changing the color of button that opens a worksheet displaying the new data. When the user opens that document, the button color returns to its original color.

Centrally-Controlled Messages

The information for triggering signal displays is stored in a database table. It exists in the form of a column holding customized "yes/no" fields for individual users and individual documents. If new information is loaded into the system, the appropriate column field will automatically be set to "yes" for all system users. When a user accesses the document containing the new information, the column field entry is automatically switched to "no." In both cases, the color-coding of the document button is driven by the "yes/no" column field entry. The color-coding logic is built directly into the information system application. As part of the formula behind the button that opens a document, an additional function is included that changes the database column field entry from "yes" to "no" (consequently changing the background color of the button) when the button is clicked.

Yet another field in this central table registers the specific theme areas about which the individual users wish to be kept informed. This additional field makes it possible to "screen out" unimportant (from the perspective of the individual user) data updates for theme areas not related to the employee's specific function role.

Periodic Queries

It makes sense to incorporate a periodic timer into the application (see page 54). The timer is used to automatically generate queries checking the status of the data in the base system, so users can be alerted to updated data as it enters the system. Generally, notification of updated data is done using color-coded document navigation buttons.

Virtual Newspaper

It is theoretically possible to set up the system so that the information display and news headlines that appear in the applications are driven by defined user IDs or user group IDs. Some companies are experimenting with this idea, though it has yet to become a standard method for designing systems. The messages could be ordered into distinct themes or theme areas, and the user would only receive messages related to those areas to which he/she has subscribed. The relevant news stories appear in the form of text headlines, which can be clicked upon to access the complete information display. This type of system user interface is the first step towards creating a corporate-wide, user group-oriented virtual newspaper (see also 190).

5.7.1.4   Standard Settings

As a general rule, the information displayed when a user opens a specific theme area module is the highest level of data available (usually figures for the corporation as a whole). Divisional or subsidiary heads can choose to directly view the data related to their specific organizational responsibilities as their initial display. Of course, they still have access to the higher-level information.

The control information that defines at what corporate level an individual user's display should open is stored centrally in a dedicated data table.

5.7.1.5   Personal Settings

Saving the menu settings that were selected the last time a document was accessed provides a more user-friendly interface, but places considerable demand on the overall system user support. A feature currently missing from inSight® that would increase its overall comfort level is the ability to automatically save the last selected menu settings in a central data table. In fact, inSight® does "remember" the numerical position of the active menu selection when an application is saved. But the available selections in data-driven menu objects are constantly changing, causing the saved numerical position to display a different menu selection. To insure that a menu selection is saved, the application menu selection attributes must be static and fixed.

Practical examples where this feature has been successfully integrated into an information system can be found in two specialized, autonomous systems. These two systems will now be briefly discussed.

Personnel
Management System

A personnel management system was developed in which a user's last menu selections and document settings are automatically saved. Since many documents have more than five display selection possibilities, it was decided to use a particular color to identify those selections for which data was available. Otherwise, it would be possible for users to select a display for which there was no data. Another feature that was built into the system is a "Start-Up Settings" button, that returns the menu selections to a specific default setting when the user clicks on it. This saves the user the time and aggravation of having to individually set the menu objects.

Cost Center
Information System

A cost center information system with countless detailed data selection possibilities was designed to automatically lead individual users back to the menu selections they used the last time they accessed the system. The system was designed to centrally store this control information. This means that the user will always be able to recall the same menu settings, regardless of what PC is used to access the system (as long as the PC is connected to the corporate network).

5.7.2 Individual PC Settings

Some control settings and information are stored locally. When viewing a raw material pricing display, the user can select an individual raw material that should be graphically displayed. When the display document is closed, the selected raw material is automatically saved. When the document is centrally updated, however, the selected raw material setting is lost.

149

Accessing Other
Applications

Using the START command, users are able to launch other programs from within an inSight® application. When the other program ends, the user is automatically brought back to the original
inSight® application. It is not always possible to transfer parameters to or pull back parameters from the launched program. But
it is possible to launch a particular program application with
stored settings and parameters. Some communication programs,
like appointment planners, fax programs or e-mail programs, naturally lend themselves to this type of usage. The true "multi-tas-
king" power of these program combinations is limited by the
lack of a true program integration mechanism (see page 88).
One feature that has managed to win widespread acceptance is
the ability to launch an Internet browser from within an application. It is recommended that the home page that appears when
the browser is launched be adapted to fit the general format and
layout of the information system itself.

In an example taken from a real system, an information system
contains a communication line with six buttons, of which five
can be individually adjusted (a list of the dates for the most important internal corporate meetings and events is simply hard-
wired to the buttons). A file stored on the PC contains the button
labels, the application (or program) paths and a message that
tells whether the function is active or not. The file can be easily
modified by a data processing employee, or even directly by the
employee.

Area Codes

The file also includes information about the physical location
where the PC is installed, so that the telephone area code can be
passed along to other corporate plant sites.

5.7.3 Application Administration

With the use of proper controlling and documentation programs,
it should be possible to develop an efficient and error-free
maintenance routine for an information system. Central to this
concept is a system overview, listing the documents in the
system, along with information related to document content responsibility, the date documents were last changed, any notes
concerning the documents, etc. A listing of which tables and
columns can be used by which documents is also helpful in
maintaining a system. This holds true for SAP®-EIS as well,
where a listing of the aspect tables used in different Reports
adds transparency to the system.

Paper-less Administration

A user table stores the dates that the different users last accessed the system. Administrative processes like requests for new users, creation of new users, and system monitoring can also be converted to a paper-less environment, with the help of a small inSight® application.

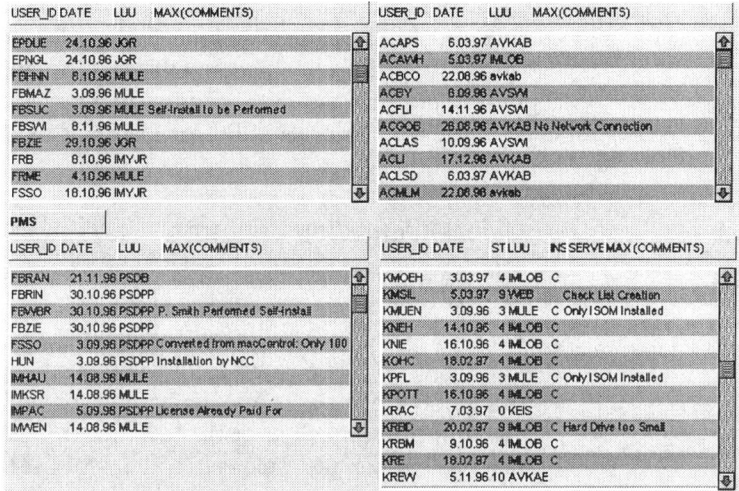

Exhibit 38: Administration Tables

Ideal Number of Tables

The ideal number and type of administration tables is difficult to determine, because this is a young subject area without much practical evidence to analyze. The following list of table types is meant to give a general idea of some common administrative strategies:

- MIS user name and address
- MIS user access privileges
- MIS user technical environment
- Personal settings (one table per subject)
- Last access for each MIS user and each document
- Listing of system deadlines
- Name and address of person responsible for data preparation
- Name and address of person responsible for data contents
- System subjects and themes
- inSight® documents, status, responsible developer
- Bug and error lists, improvements

5.7.4   Expansions and Errors

When errors or suggestions for expanded functions surface, and these suggestions can not be immediately or easily implemented in the application, it is a good idea to develop an internal timeline for undertaking changes to the application. As an application proves its stability and reliability, access to it can be expanded within the corporation. The bug fixes and expanded features that arcplan programmers have planned for inSight® are of particular interest. The system used by arcplan, similar to the system used by the majority of corporate application developers, is based on a prioritized list for fixes and new functions.

5.8   Global Information Concept

The already extensive use of corporate-wide information systems can be seen as the first step in developing a global information concept. One of the key precepts of a global information concept is to move away from the torrents of paper information that flood managers' desks daily, and toward a system based on electronic information display. At the moment, the employees responsible for the editorial content of electronic systems lack the experience to properly develop and care for such systems. There is hope, however, that developments in easy-to-use Internet programs will lead to breakthroughs that are directly applicable in global information systems.

Step-by-Step Plan for Developing an Intranet

Very few large corporations have developed a step-by-step plan for establishing a corporate Intranet. The central data processing department is responsible for corporate networks, but they usually only act when a request is sent by a specific division. It is difficult to develop a plausible Intranet concept outside of the data processing group, because the technical expertise of a company is concentrated in the data processing group. Even the employees in the data processing department have some problems working with this new medium. Most data processing employees are used to working with "traditional" data processing techniques, centered around logically-developed base systems and the supporting structures they require.

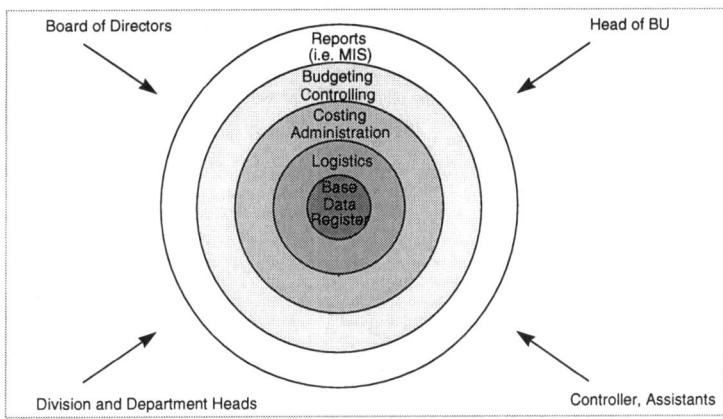

Exhibit 39: Data Processing Focuses

The data processing group is particularly interested in the inner circles, specifically the base data, logistic, administration and invoicing systems. They are not as well-equipped to deal with planning and controlling systems. They have even less contact with information systems. Many corporate employees incorrectly view the data processing department simply as data suppliers for the real decision-makers. Because the true strengths of the data processing department are not easily recognized by outsiders, many employees have a less than positive impression of what they do. The data processing department views itself as the data administrator, and is often reluctant to take on responsibility for the actual data contents. They are therefore generally opposed to taking on the role of an "information supplier." On the other hand, data processing is literally the only department capable of fulfilling this role, due to the lack of technical knowledge in the other departments.

Information
Distribution as an
Independent
Function

A global information concept eliminates this inherent tension and conflict. The data processing-supported information distribution must become a separate corporate department. It is crucial, at least during the learning phase, that this department have full access to all corporate technical resources. Without detailed knowledge of the information structure (which can only come from practical experience), there is little hope for success in mastering the complex technical demands of a global information system.

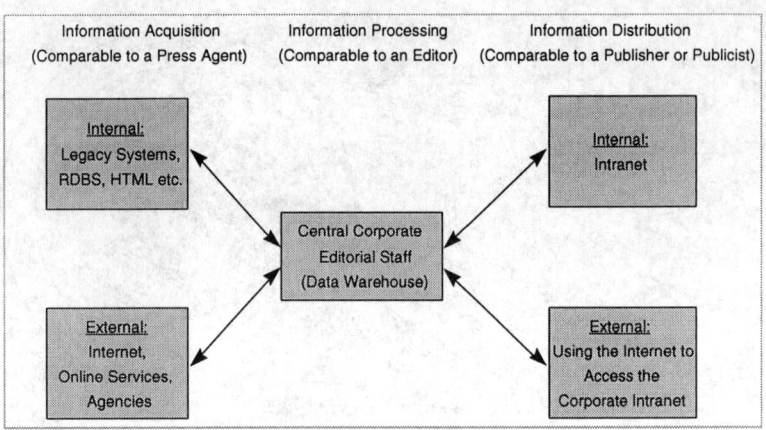

| Information Acquisition (Comparable to a Press Agent) | Information Processing (Comparable to an Editor) | Information Distribution (Comparable to a Publisher or Publicist) |

Exhibit 40: Corporate Information Structure

A logical development would be the creation of a "corporate information" unit, responsible for providing information via an Intranet. A central editorial staff insures that the information available is reliable and constantly updated. To achieve synergistic benefits, it makes sense to assign editorial responsibilities to the people or department who are currently responsible for distributing information (albeit in paper form) internally and externally.

Easy Access

The "Intranet technique" differs from traditional mediums like newspaper and television mediums in its easy accessibility to all information. This includes source data and other information that in the past has been unavailable or difficult to find. Every Internet user has direct access to an unbelievably large number of information sources. When dealing with an Internet/Intranet environment, quantity does not guarantee quality. Often times, the massive amounts of available data are more confusing than helpful. A good strategy is to offer centrally-edited information, along with links to related or interesting Internet sites.

The information prepared for the Intranet is available and accessible in the same format and style as Internet information. From a technical perspective, an Intranet is simply an additional piece of the Internet. Access to an Intranet, however, is limited to company employees.

Interaction

Another important feature that sets Internet/Intranet applications apart from traditional information mediums is interactivity: In principle, every Internet/Intranet user is able to have a dialog with the information provider. There are already a number of Internet web servers offering this service. It is clear that this option will have an enormous (and positive) influence on the corporate information landscape.

Java versus ActiveX

The success of the Internet has pushed HTML technology (which serves as the basis for building web servers) into the foreground of modern computing. HTML will have a profound impact on other technologies, like the two level client/server architecture commonly found in information systems and other similar applications. It doesn't make sense today to convert existing information systems to HTML, or to rebuild systems with Java programs. A better solution is to make MIS applications directly "Internet/Intranet capable." This means that, like HTML documents, the information system can be viewed and used with a PC Internet browser (see ActiveX technology from Microsoft, page 180).

5.9   Critical Success Factors

5.9.1   Layout

An attractive optical appearance can have a significant positive impact on the overall acceptance of an information system. It makes sense to consult with internal advertising personnel, in order to incorporate elements of the firm-specific "corporate identity" into the program. A positive side effect of these discussions is an implicit internal credibility with regards to the system layout. It is then easier to brush aside minor and unproductive layout criticisms from individual users (see page 118).

Care should be taken not to use to many colors in the information system user interface. Bright or loud colors should only be used to draw attention to exception reports or special system functions. Data lists are often easier to read on a computer screen if an alternating two-color pattern is used for the list. The use of the corporate logo, at the very least on the start-up screen, usually makes the system less intimidating for users. It also lends a sense of official acceptance of the system, helping to win credibility with end users.

When printing (print displays usually correspond one to one with screen displays), screen control elements like screen navigation buttons or print command buttons can be removed from the print display. To do this, the "don't print" option should be selected for the control elements. Unfortunately, it is not possible to print objects defined as "invisible" (like titles, date cells, or time cells). Thus, in some cases special print worksheets will need to be defined. For the best optical impression, the print output should be defined to automatically fill the page format layout. For a quick print, or for printing on a black-and-white printer, the color printing features can be switched off.

5.9.2 User Interface

The design and layout of the user interface plays a key role in end user acceptance of an application. Some developers believe that a mouse-driven user interface automatically guarantees user-friendly applications. This is unfortunately not the case. A mouse-driven interface is of little help if the layout and naming convention for menus and control buttons is confusing.

Intuitive Application Development

One sometimes has the impression that the software programmers forgot how hard it is for untrained users to work with their program. A user must often devote large amounts of time and energy to fully grasp the true benefits a program offers. Handbooks and online help are the second-best method for teaching new users. The best way to train users (and win their acceptance) is to develop a program that operates intuitively.

Less is More

Many software programs are judged on the breadth and width of functions they offer. With information systems, the major emphasis is on user-friendliness. For the end user, as few functions as possible should be available. In many cases, the four standard function buttons in inSight®'s user mode ("End," "Print," "Back to Start-up Sheet," and "One Navigation Step Back") offer the user enough control over the application.

The user interface needs to be so good that a training session is superfluous. The user should not notice any data processing aspects of the program. Key Styleguide elements, like hints for sorting lists (see page 119), need to be designed and placed in such a way that the user is able to recognize their importance. Even if the user is unable to fully comprehend the features or uses of these functions, they should be designed so that the user can easily experiment with them. It can be helpful to have a system where the cursor symbol changes when it passes over an object, based on the function defined for the object. In addition to detailed functional hints, "shortcuts" should also be available, so that experienced users can quickly begin to work with the program.

An interesting issue is the so-called "navigation through multidimensional data" (see page 7). Spectacular drilldown technologies and unlimited data dimension navigation are more appropriate for analysts and controllers. For normal users, the use of these technologies should be limited and targeted.

Fun

These points are meant to make the user less afraid of an application, and (in so far as it is possible) to make the application fun to use. An application is much more likely to be accepted if users are proud of it, and feel comfortable using it.

5.9.3   Current Data

Monthly data is eagerly anticipated when it is first released. After that, most managers quickly lose interest in it. An information system that uses data released on a monthly basis will not likely generate much interest, except on the first couple of days of every month when the updated data is first available.

Available in System First; then on Paper

If users are able to access the new data in paper form a day or two before the electronic data is released to the system (which is not an uncommon occurrence in many information systems), it is highly unlikely that the information system will experience high usage and enjoy long-term corporate success. In fact, the system will probably wither and die from a lack of managerial support.

If it is impossible to eliminate a parallel paper information system, system developers should at least make sure that the on-line information is more current than the paper information. This is not always easy to do, especially with the widespread popularity and use of fax machines. Another advantage of fax transmissions is the fact that the sender is able to attach commentaries or insights related to the transmitted data. To insure usage of the electronic system, the information distribution process can be organized in such a way that alternative distribution systems are forbidden. Such measures will not guarantee the success of a computerized information system. In order to win support and be successful, the electronic system needs to be easy-to-use, and offer the most current information available.

Bells and Whistles

The importance of having the most up-to-date data in an information system is obvious. But is equally important for the system to include "bells and whistles" features that attract the interest and attention of the end users. A good example is a constantly-updated news ticker, so that users have an incentive to stay linked to the system. A good system uses a periodic timer (usually set to trigger every two to five minutes) to retrieve new news stories or update items like stock prices, and announces the new information on the system start-up page (see page 148).

5.9.4   **Speed**

Acceptable response times lie between one and five seconds. In some cases, a response time of eight to ten seconds is acceptable (i.e. when data for several attribute combinations is retrieved in a single query). The advantage to defining such queries is that the application does not need to continuously access data from the central server. When the data is retrieved from the PC's main memory, the application performance is faster.

Too Broadly-Defined Reports

When using SAP®-EIS, in which reports are generated in the main memory of the server (see page 95), broadly-defined reports can lead to time problems in generating the initial report. After the report is generated, application response times will be very fast. The initial report generation time can be improved by saving the report on the server's hard drive. The system administrator can activate this option.

Designing an application is a tight-rope walk between high user comfort and fast response times. Filling document menus with data is a particular response time trouble area. The actual data query is usually very fast, and takes up less than 10 % of the total response time. In the systems developed to date using inSight®, the emphasis has almost always been on user-friendliness over response times.

Other Performance Constraints

There are a number of other factors (some over which the developer has no control) which can negatively influence the performance of a client/server application. The most common complaints are network problems and over-burdened servers. The consequences of these problems can be catastrophic: Since the ODBC connection to DB2 relational databases is synchronous, the PC simply delivers control of the query to the database, and then "waits" until the database answers. Sometimes the waiting time is several minutes long, especially if changes are being made to the table structure. If such problems regularly occur, organizational measures need to be taken to insure that major database work is not done during normal working hours.

5.9.5   Stability

Client-server applications often use a number of different components from a number of different vendors. Technology developments have largely removed the application instabilities associated with multiple vendor components. Most client PC programs now run completely problem-free. The only serious problems that still occasionally appear are related to PC memory devices. The real problems that everyday users may encounter are network problems and central database server problems. Given the current technology state, users can expect a system to suffer a complete shutdown (for up to several hours) about twice a month. Users can also expect query times to vary, sometimes taking a few seconds and sometimes several minutes. The source of this discrepancy is not always clear, so it is a good idea to record performance variations and problems in a problem log.

5.9.6   Quantifiable Benefits

Paper Flood

Large corporations employ a number of employees whose primary responsibilities are related to information distribution. Their tasks include printing reports, packaging them, and sending them to the appropriate managers and analysts. Considerable effort is expended to insure that the information arrives where and when it should, and more effort is used to register and (sometimes) time-stamp receipt of the documents. Often times, copies of the information are made and distributed to superiors, coworkers, and colleagues. Some "less critical" documents are passed around according to a hierarchical distribution list. The danger with these systems is that the documents could get lost, or arrive too late to be acted upon.

Hard to Evaluate Economic Benefits

It will be several years before this costly and time-consuming process can be completely replaced by a data processing-supported information system. Until then, cost/use calculations comparing these two processes are not real useful. For one thing, it is very difficult to identify and properly value all the costs associated with the internal gathering, processing and distribution of the information. Another issue is the fact that the existing information distribution process will be somewhat optimized (through years of trial and error experience), but this infrastructure needs to be developed and built (at considerable cost) for the information system. In addition to connecting office PCs to the system via a high performance network, there is also a need for an "on the move" solution. Equipping employees with note-book computers remains a possible but expensive option.

5.9.7   Non-Quantifiable Benefits

Despite the costs of a quick implementation plan, it is not a good idea to use a gradual migration plan to move to a data pro-cessing-supported information distribution system. In addition to the technical requirements, there are also hurdles to overcome related to the mental and organizational changes necessary for a successful migration.

Increased
Transparency

The non-quantifiable benefits to a company of a data processing department-supported information acquisition process can not be overemphasized. System data is more accurate and is able to reach users faster. The company's information processing be-comes more transparent to end users and management. The pro-blem of having several different numbers from several different sources for the same data query is greatly reduced. Many compa-nies have already recognized these non-quantifiable benefits, and are working towards integrating this concept into their infor-mation system strategies.

Direct contact with business information structures empowers managers (for the first time) to effectively guide and analyze the actions and support of the data processing department. Their fear of using the new programs and applications will start to dis-appear. Corporate decision-makers are once again willing to tackle important information system issues, instead of automa-tically deferring authority to the resident "data processing guru."

Understanding
Relationships

By forcing managers to better understand the relationships that drive their reporting structures and business models, a positive "side effect" emerges. Namely, the involvement of the data pro-cessing department enables managers to improve these proces-ses and make them more cost effective. Also, by better under-standing relationships and structures, it is easier for corporations to institute important re-engineering measures. Managerial atten-tion is then freed to concentrate on learning how to interface with the new system technologies, which is another non-quanti-fiable system benefit.

5.9.8 Costs, Economic Viability

The costs of implementing an information system can vary depending on the existing data system structures within a company. The largest cost factor is the preparation of data. Data must often be culled from base operative systems, and registers need to be coordinated with each other. The costs associated with this infrastructure development result in ancillary benefits as well, as they increase coordination between various corporate business units and departments. Further, they make it easier to create systems and applications that display information spanning these business units and departments. Unfortunately, there are few (if any) companies that have separate cost accounts for these expenditures. For this reason, it is not easy to develop an unfailing system for assessing the true costs of establishing the necessary infrastructure.

Automatic Data Supply

A well-designed corporate information system is based on a reliable, automated raw data retrieval process, which limits the system administrator's need to manually enter or modify data. Such a system can be maintained by one or two employees, who are also able to continue developing new application modules. The total costs of this structure to a large corporation (with several hundred end users) generally fall between $250,000 and 350,000 per year.

The actual costs related to the programming of the application are considerably smaller. Assuming that an adequate data structure is already in place, an experienced developer can create a user-ready application module in as little as two work days. An additional work day should be factored into the equation, so the developer can create documentation for the application. Pure application maintenance costs are negligible. Adding new functions to an application requires a bit more time and energy, but this cost is generally offset by the increased analysis capabilities provided to the end users.

Only the User can Evaluate the Total System Benefits

Trying to evaluate the total financial benefits of an information system is an impossible task. Only a user who is actively involved with the system on a regular basis can estimate the value of his or her own personal benefits. But because most corporations today already have a decent reporting system in place (usually in the form of paper reports), it is possible to do a rough comparison of the general costs associated with different reporting forms. As was mentioned above, however, simply taking these comparisons at face value can be misleading. A corporation is therefore advised to develop a cost budget for the development of a data processing-supported information system, and not to try to calculate the total overall costs and benefits of the system. More and more employees are coming to view corporate information as a "product." Unfortunately, most companies have yet to start handling information like a "product." There is no form of pecuniary measurement for information. The commonly-used method of charging users based on the number of central server processing seconds each information request requires ignores the actual value of the information being transmitted. The only true method for gauging the value of different bits of corporate information is by establishing a "payment" system (see also page 188). Most corporations appear to be miles away from recognizing this fact. The technical design of the ideal information system should include the ability to eliminate or temporarily suspend "information prices" if this becomes necessary for winning system support.

6 Maintaining an Information System

6.1 Organization

6.1.1 "System Manager"

An information system requires constant attention and care. Although the individual corporate divisions are responsible for the accuracy of the system's information, users generally want the system to have a general contact person. The contact person is the one users call with questions, complaints and compliments. It is the contact person who has the ultimate responsibility for insuring that the system is always "up and running."

Missing Job
Description

Unfortunately, there is no corresponding job description for this position in any of the popular information system guides and books available today. One is hard-pressed to find a description of the responsibilities of a Data Warehouse manager. A basic job description for this position should include:

- Data Storage
  - Establishing the data structure
  - Optimizing the data structure (Performance)
- Content Model
  - Coordinating data contents with data suppliers
  - Describing and controlling contents
- Module Library
  - Creating and improving analysis modules
  - Distributing analysis modules
- Maintaining the Data Warehouse
  - Creating tables
  - Coordinating deadlines with data suppliers
  - Maintaining the server
- Administration and Documentation
  - Creating/maintaining user perspectives
  - Creating an information catalog
  - Cost accounting for "customers" and "suppliers"

A possible explanation for these missing job descriptions can be traced to the fact that most hardware and software suppliers recommend instituting a fully-automated system. As far as they are concerned, the subject of a system manager is therefore irrelevant. In reality, the responsibilities and obligations tied to the position of "system manager" are the issues that can make or break a corporate-wide information system.

Publishing a Virtual Newspaper

The day to day administration of an information system is very similar to the day to day running of a newspaper. Any rational person can readily see that there are no "intelligent" computers available to publishers that are capable of searching the news wires and automatically putting together the daily editions. The same holds true for "publishing" an information system, only in this case the editor is called the "system manager."

The term "Data Warehouse" does not completely describe the requirements for gathering, storing, and processing the data used in an information system. Users can not (nor should they be expected to) simply "pull" data from the warehouse. Staying with this metaphor, there is no "self service;" instead, the users' access to the Data Warehouse is restricted to communication through the information system. All user interfaces, therefore, occur along clearly structured information channels. The user never has direct contact with the Data Warehouse tables. In fact, it is likely that the user will have no knowledge of their existence.

Business Information Shop

The term "Business Information Shop" (see page 40) describes this situation better. Following this terminology, the Data Warehouse is a storage facility for the Business Information Shop. It is not necessary for one person to centrally control all the information system functions, but the system manager should be aware of all the system components and supervise system activities.

There is no reasonable justification for a large corporation building an Information Shop without taking any preparatory measures. Such an undertaking is doomed to failure from the start, for a variety of reasons. Large companies should strive to develop smaller, meaningful projects, so employees can gain the experience needed to build a successful corporate-wide Information Shop. To this end, the use of central and specific Information Shops can be helpful.

Central Information Shops distribute the calculation results of the operative systems, most notably profit and cost figures. They are also responsible for providing critical data about outstanding orders, inventory levels and personnel issues. Providing access to market research data is yet another responsibility of centralized corporate information suppliers. On the other side, specific Information Shops provide more detailed information about the operative data for individual (or related groups of) corporate areas. Examples of specific Information Shops include customer information, business analyses for specific divisions, excerpts of strategic and logistical directives, and minutes from pertinent executive council and project team meetings.

It would be silly to leave the development and maintenance of these Business Information Shops completely unregulated. The development process and use of terminology needs to be synchronized at a centralized level. This will not only eliminate wasteful parallel development, but will also reduce the amount of confusion regarding the definition of data records and how they are to be interpreted. A popular and effective means to achieving cohesiveness within Business Information Shops is the use of "system standards," which lay down corporate guidelines for all the individual shops.

The "system standards" should address:

- The construction and maintenance of a superordinate, multilingual catalog of terms
- The definition of the Business Information Shop content and functional requirements
- Suggestions for the structure and organization of the Business Information Shop (plan of action)
- The definition of the information processing requirements (including the necessary application tools)
- The definition of the information display requirements (Styleguide)
- Guidelines for operating a Business Information Shop (operating handbook)
- The availability of demonstration examples
- Bibliography

Constantly Changing Structures

Modern corporations are constantly changing organizational and reporting structures. An information system must be dynamic enough to be able to accommodate and reflect these changes.

165

Many of these changes are data-driven, and the system can easily adapt to such changes. However, there are also more substantial infrastructure changes which require fast and decisive action. It is important that the policy for implementing system changes be flexible and free of bureaucracy.

It is truly surprising how many good ideas spring from the system users. Most of their ideas are minor application modifications that are easy to implement. When such ideas surface, they should be implemented quickly, without being submitted to a bureaucratic decision-making process. In line with this concept, a successful "system manager," will have direct access to and (at least some) control over the technology used in the Business Information Shop.

To be able to perform the job, the "system manager" needs to have extensive knowledge related to the system contents as well as the system's technical aspects. It is not easy to find an employee with the education and practical experience necessary to fulfill the job requirements. Making the position even harder to fill is the fact that environmental factors (chances for promotions, ability to showcase one's talents for upper management) inherently discourage ambitious employees from considering the job. Managing and administering an information system is still considered a second tier position that is more likely to hurt than help one's career chances.

6.1.2   Content Manager

Like every other production facility, the Business Information Shop should enter into contracts with its "raw material" suppliers. A good idea is to designate a "content manager" for every Business Information Shop theme. This person is also responsible for answering any end user questions related to his or her theme area. The "content manager" should generally hold an important or visible position within the department. The department manager should carefully choose the "content manager," along with a corresponding "preparation manager."

Data Delivery
Responsibilities

The concept of a "content manager" has proven to be a valuable part of a functional information system in company after company. One of the reasons for this is that the "content manager" lends credibility to the system in the eyes of the data suppliers. The true goal of the system, however, is to push more and more responsibility for the system down to the level of the data

suppliers. Ideally, this will lead to the development of an autonomous Business Information Shop (see page 40).

6.1.3   Preparation Manager

The "preparation manager, " as the name suggests, is responsible
for insuring that complete and reliable data is available to the
system managers by the established deadline. Like the previously
discussed "content managers," preparation managers are appoin-
ted by the various department heads.

The evolution of this position reflects the current trend towards
transferring Data Warehouse activities to the department responsible for the information content. The widespread acceptance
of this trend weakens any arguments that favor a centralized
Data Warehouse. In fact, many companies are now experimenting with the idea of having their individual departments (instead
of the centralized IT department) create the actual application
modules. The necessary corporate-wide technical and layout
coordination is taken care of through the earlier-described
"system standards." Using these principles, the information
system becomes a collection of various theme areas, with each
area representing a business module. A large portion of the
"system manager's" responsibility is delegated to the information-
providing departments. It is not a good idea to try to implement
this organizational structure when the information system is in its
conceptual or early development stages; instead it should be
introduced after the system's theme areas have been expanded
to encompass a broad range of corporate reporting needs. Until
the system reaches that point, details related to the form and
transmission of system data should be handled by a designated
"system manager."

Under this concept, the "preparation manager" decides how to
define and retrieve the data from his or her department. When
the time comes to create a "data pipe line," the preparation
manager can of course expect expert support from the "system
manager." After all, it is in the system manager's interest to
develop an automated data delivery and processing routine for
the system's various modules.

6.1.4   Involving the Office Staff

At first view, it may seem silly to devote a separate section of this book to this issue. But experiences to date have proved how valuable the involvement of the office staff can be to the long-term success of an information system.

It is very important to involve the secretaries in the project, especially if management is not using PCs at the time the project is introduced. Installing computers in the bosses' offices can cause the secretaries to emotionally reject the system, out of a fear of the new technology and worries about how it will alter the existing work environment. They believe that the new technology will lessen their input and contributions to the company. Once these fears surface, it is very difficult to explain them away, even with intense, individual discussions.

Responsibly Involve
Office Staff

An effective strategy is to responsibly involve the office staff in system support functions. They should be the first reference source when questions, problems or suggestions arise. Many technical difficulties can be manually corrected with little disruption or effort. For example, re-starting the computer can bring the system back up if it has frozen up on the user. An informed office staff can handle small problems like this without having to call in a system service technician.

In one actual system implementation, the office staff was given a couple weeks to familiarize themselves with the system before the system was rolled out to the intended end users. The system administrators simultaneously helped to build a PC infrastructure for the entire department. To insure continued satisfaction with the system, and also as a gesture of thanks, the system administrators still have a dedicated hotline for the secretaries. They can use the hotline to get answers to any questions or problems related to the PCs as well as to get help with the system (see also page 140).

When a deliberate strategy is used to involve the office staff, they often turn out to be the best source for getting user feedback. This is essential to enabling quick reaction times for system problems. If these issues are not dealt with quickly, they can fester and lead to user dissatisfaction. Positive feedback lets the developers and administrators know that they are on the right track, and can serve as a motivational source for further development and enhancements.

6.1.5 Involving Assistants

It goes against common wisdom to intentionally limit the role of assistants and controllers in the initial phases of building an information system. Their knowledge and experience in generating reports is valuable, but this is often due to the fact that they are the only employees able to navigate the jungle of data stored in the corporate databases. As such, the task of creating and maintaining a corporate reporting system often falls on them by default. Since assistants and controllers lack comprehensive database skills, they generally use PC programs like Microsoft Office products to download and locally process data. The fruits of their labor are usually presented (in table or graph form) in paper reports or in computerized systems designed for small user groups. These reports and systems do not include the ability to modify existing data or transmit new data to the central database tables.

Many large corporations are beginning to recognize the value of information system administrators. The data processing department-supported report generator position has become more popular as central relational databases have become more popular. The key to these new systems is the periodic retrieval of data from the operative base systems (see page 30).

An information system has far-reaching effects on the employees within the divisions and departments where it is deployed. A commonly-heard sentiment is the fear that the new information system will eventually accomplish the work for which these employees are currently responsible.

Chance for
Controllers and
Assistants

There is no doubt that an information system can substantially reduce the amount of time needed to gather and format data needed for important analyses and presentations. There is also no doubt that the system may alienate employees who assess their own value to the corporation based on their ability to perform these gathering and formatting tasks. But one must assume that the affected assistants and controllers will quickly adapt to the new technologies introduced by an information system. After all, they end up with more time to devote to the true focus of their work: Analyzing corporate data and adding their expert observations to the total corporate data pool.

Real-life attempts to integrate assistants and controllers into total corporate information system concepts have proven how difficult this task truly is. Their traditional focus on a limited user group prevents them from recognizing and implementing "big picture" data analyses. Emancipating these employees from the tedious, formalized procedures of the data processing department provides them with a sense of self-confidence that is both liberating and dangerous. Ten controllers from ten different departments will likely develop ten different technical solutions to a single reporting issue. Compounding the problem is the wide selection of management information systems available on the market today, most of which are specifically targeted at aiding assistants and controllers in their everyday work routine.

Mentality Change

The importance of changing the typical assistant and controller mentality towards information systems can not be stressed enough. History has shown that assistants and controllers tend to (oftentimes unintentionally) hijack IT projects, or torpedo efforts to implement new information systems. Regardless of which scenario was played out, the probability of project success shrank dramatically. In the past, the building of a corporate-wide information system by the controlling department led to competitive resentments within other departments. As a result, these systems never enjoyed widespread user support and acceptance.

Of course, there are always exceptions. But in many cases, the data processing and controlling departments just don't get along anymore. Each department uses their own jargon and euphemisms, which intentionally or unintentionally create hurdles to inter-departmental communication. Everyone is forced to resort to tedious and complicated procedures like defining system requirements and system specifications (see page 75) in order to achieve common goals. Frequently heard sentences like "the users don't know what they want" or "the data processing department doesn't understand our business" add to the overall tension. Perhaps an information system should be viewed as a chance to bury past differences, and advance exchanges and discourse between these groups. To be successful, the system needs to include the expert competencies of both of these groups.

Molding a focused, committed team out of the employees coming from these two completely different worlds is one of the most formidable challenges to building and maintaining an information system.

6.2   Creating a Productive Application

6.2.1   Developing A New Module

6.2.1.1   Dimension-Hierarchy Definition

If the data that is to be used in an application can be ordered into different dimensions and hierarchy levels, it is a good idea to create a description of this multidimensional data cube. A business module built on the basis of this description can only display the contents and related identification codes contained in the data cube. If user expectations for the system are unrealistic, this module can be used as a basis for explaining what is and is not possible. An example can be seen on page 14.

Rarely More Than Eight Dimensions

One rarely finds a real-life example where more than eight dimensions are used. Some software vendors brag of models where 20 or more dimensions are used, but they count hierarchical levels as individual dimensions. While this semantic subtlety may sound more impressive, it also serves to confuse and mislead consumers.

6.2.1.2   Data Usefulness Analysis

The real usefulness of various types of data has been discussed throughout this book. Thinking of data as being either correct or incorrect ignores deeper, structural issues related to an information system. Actual occurrences of "incorrect" numeric data are rare. But when data is pulled from multiple data sources, and the system simply compares figures from one data source with figures from another, there exists the very real danger that the system is comparing like but not identical data. Even consolidated data, where intra-corporate transactions are eliminated, can cause corporate sales figures to appear to be different from business unit sales figures, where intra-corporate transactions are included.

Lack of Practical Formalism

To date, no practical formalism has emerged for structuring the analysis of data usefulness. Until more detailed data and relevant studies become available, companies will continue to have to rely on non-scientific surveys of target users to determine what data is considered useful. The development and execution of these surveys should include input from the system's designated "content manager" (see page 166). If the survey results indicate that the system design is unlikely to provide "useful" (from the end user perspective) data, adjustments need to be made to the system. Under a best case scenario, the data can be edited or the layout designs reformatted to meet user expectations. The adjustment process can take much longer if the information sources need to be modified. In addition to possible technical difficulties, there is also a strong chance that interpersonal problems will surface. The administrators of the information source systems are unlikely to understand, sympathize with, or be willing to undertake the necessary changes needed to bring their successful systems in compliance with a non-existent or unproven MIS.

6.2.1.3   Data Availability Analysis

Like the analysis of data usefulness, the analysis of data availability is difficult to formalize. There is simply not enough gathered data on the subject. The overriding goal of the analysis must be to impress the importance of data availability on the "data preparer(s)." System developers should strive towards a system whose data acquisition is supported by the data processing department. Also, the system should move as quickly as possible from manual data preparation to an automated electronic data transfer.

At the conclusion of an analysis with positive results, it is recommended that a "data delivery contract" be worked out with the employees responsible for preparing the system data (see page 167). The contract should include exact specifications relating to the quality, type, extent and deadlines for data delivery.

6.2.1.4   Prototyping

Attempts to diagram user interfaces in the form of system requirements have been an unquestionable failure. The end users and their data processing representatives can not comprehend the full power of a software product like inSight®, so their system suggestions often fail to extend beyond a simple "two dimensional" display. Developers on the other hand, are capable of sitting down with users and creating operational (albeit unrefined) data display screens that utilize the capabilities in the chosen software package. The only task that remains after application prototypes are put together is to optimize the display and technical data retrieval aspects of the various documents. This process is a departure from the "normal" system development route, where the entire system is defined in great detail before development begins, and the developer is forced to strictly adhere to the established design guidelines. The developer moves into a new role as a designer, who is responsible for suggesting possibilities to the intended system end users. With a little practice and experience, this system has proved to be very effective. Regular information exchanges with other developers can also be used to broaden developers' knowledge bases and to enhance the overall prototyping procedure. It is also a good idea to supplement conventional information exchange discussions with online discussion forums and "experience libraries" that are accessible to all developers. A uniform corporate development guide (see page 118) is the best solution for standardizing frequently-used development tactics and tricks. Yet another recommended measure is the creation of a "Styleguide clearing house," where applications from all corporate business units and departments are revised in accordance with the corporate Styleguide rules. This is often necessary because, even though developers may be following the uniform layout form requirements, minor layout differences and variations always occur.

Positive Practical Experiences

All the procedures and processes described above have proven to be durable and effective. In particular, the conscious decision not to use a set of system requirements has proven to be advantageous for overall system development and implementation. Along these lines, it is interesting to note the difficulty associated with creating an "after the fact" handbook for a comprehensive information system. The energy and resources needed to document and describe all the possible data displays are so costly as to be unjustifiable. If it is so difficult to document the system even after it has been developed, it is clear that it would be almost impossible to document the system (specifically through the use of system requirements or system specifications) before the development phase begins.

Successful information systems built using the operative system development method (see page 75) are extremely rare. There is still hope that the iterative process of using dimension-hierarchy definitions, the analysis of data usefulness and the analysis of data availability (see pages 171 and 172) will be able to gain acceptance in large corporations, and become part of their standard data processing repertoire.

6.2.2   Rules For Developing inSight® Models

When developing inSight® applications, the following points should be considered:

- When developing applications that are to run on both Windows and APPLE Macintosh computers, the font selection becomes important. The Arial font has proven to be an effective combination font. In general, the row height in column and row objects should be defined by the developer. Otherwise, it is possible that differences in the automatic setting of these two platforms will occur.
- Document file names should be clearly and uniquely identifiable, especially in larger applications (see page 125).
- If possible, scroll bars should be avoided in document objects.
- It is very easy to get carried away and define a number of formulas in a number of inSight® objects triggered by a number of different events. There is a very real danger to this, because an application can quickly grow very complicated and hard to modify. If an identical formula is defined in several different objects (for example, if a sort formula for a table object is defined in multiple cell objects), the developer must change the formula in all these objects if a new or modified condition is added to the formula. It is much easier (especially for those employees who must work on the application at a later date) to define the formula in a separate, clearly-labeled button. The formula can be defined to trigger when a user clicks on the button, with the help of the EXECUTE function (see page 66).
- Instead of using constant text displays in documents, the application should use as much query-driven labeling as possible.
- Care should be taken when working with connection and repository files (see page 63). inSight® stores the connection parameters in the connection file. Special information, like how inSight® should interpret table column contents, are stored in the repository file. A connection file can only be linked with one repository file. The local inSight® database operates in a slightly different manner: File interpretation information is stored in the connection file, not in the repository file. This is an important consideration when porting Windows applications to a Macintosh computer, because the connection files are operating system

specific. When porting applications that use a relational database, this problem does not exist.

Corporate-Wide Repository Files

- When dealing with a repository file, the question arises of whether it should be created in the form of a unified corporate-wide standard, or whether the corporation should use a system of individual repository files. Convincing arguments can be made for using both of these strategies. A unified repository forces all developers to establish and follow a single set of guidelines. If this technique is realistically possible, an organization should choose this route. It should be mentioned, however, that the inSight® program lacks support functions for comparing or combining two or more repository files. The pragmatic alternative to a single repository file is the use of individual repository files. To keep the number of repository files manageable, each developer group should be limited to using a single repository file. Under no circumstances should each application module be assigned its own connection and repository files. The danger that the complete system will become too bulky and confusing is simply too high.

6.2.3 Testing an Application

Because of inSight®'s modular building process, applications can be quickly and easily tested. Functional problems generally occur only in complicated application constructions. Fortunately, these errors rarely result in incorrect data displays (which would be fatal for the system), but instead fall under the category of "beauty flaws." When actual data errors occur, they can usually be traced back to the database.

Experienced Test People

A true application test should include users with different information needs, and should be run on as many different PCs as is possible. The ideal test person is an experienced, trustworthy, and open-minded user ("minesweeper"). They should understand that the testing process is a trade-off: On the one had they are given early access to a powerful data analysis system. On the other, they should be prepared to deal with glitches and problems related to the introduction and fine-tuning of the system.

More careful testing must be done when new communication software or new inSight® versions are introduced. Past experiences with new version introductions have sometimes been less than pleasant. A good strategy is to do extensive internal testing before releasing a new software version to end users. Distributing inSight® upgrades to corporate users should be limited to once or twice a year. On a more reassuring note, the likelihood of major programming errors in the software is very low. After more than two years of productive corporate usage, any program bugs or errors that are discovered tend to be minor, and are usually related to less important program functions.

6.2.4   Object Libraries

One of the exceptional inSight® features is the ability to centrally store and administer objects and object groups (layouts) in object libraries. For every object, up to nine format and two content properties can be globally stored (see also page 53).

Storing Entire
Function Groups

One of the biggest advantages of an object library is the "re-usability" of stored objects. Continuing along this line of thinking, entire function groups can be stored, and then combined as necessary to build an application. Development times are thereby drastically reduced, and the likelihood of a development error is significantly reduced. When all these factors are considered, it becomes clear that inSight®'s object library makes it possible for less technically-knowledgeable employees to develop applications.

The implications of inSight®'s simplified development environment (and especially the use of object libraries) are colossal. Still, this function has been virtually ignored in the application examples used in this book. The reason for this is the added application risks brought on by global objects. For example, if an object library is destroyed, applications using objects from that library can no longer be opened. Even worse is the fact that these applications can't be repaired. This drawback, along with the inability to deactivate global storage features, should cause the developer to think twice about how often and in what situations the use of global objects is really necessary.

On the other hand, the use of object libraries as standardized Styleguide elements is strongly recommended. They should be available to every developer. Standardized Styleguides and layouts can be copied and used (without the above-described global link) as often as needed. Of course, using this technique also eliminates the ability to centrally administer and change application Styleguides and layouts.

6.2.5

Documentation

Scripts

inSight® supports a number of documentation functions. Using the DOCUMENTSCRIPT function, it is possible to create a list of all document objects and their corresponding properties and formulas. This function can only be used with individual documents, not with entire applications. When dealing with complex documents, the lists it creates are sometimes very long and confusing. REPOSITORYSCRIPT displays the database definitions associated with different inSight® objects. This includes aliases (see page 63) for automatically combining columns with different names from different tables, and information regarding how different columns' contents are to be interpreted by inSight®.

The CREATE SCRIPT functions records all the processes executed in the use of an application, and the time required to complete each process. It has proven beneficial to use the information in this file to modify the Report definitions in SAP®-EIS, or to change the definition of indexes in a relational table. The resulting improvements in system response times can go a long way towards generating support for the system.

The scripts alone do not provide complete and total documentation for an application. It makes sense to design the application so that the actions and processes it executes are transparent to the developer and user. This makes it easier to maintain and document the features and functions in an application.

3 Help Levels

inSight® includes three help "levels" within every application document. The primary purpose of the levels are to hide help objects that are needed for the primary document display but should not be displayed themselves. Objects can be moved from the document display to a help level and vice-versa, so that developers can first develop a document, and then later worry about grouping related objects together and labeling their functional purposes. The picture below displays an excerpt from a help level. By consciously choosing to use a clear and concise organizational structure for documents, it is easier to modify and debug the documents. It also makes it easier for new developers to quickly understand the logic behind the document display.

177

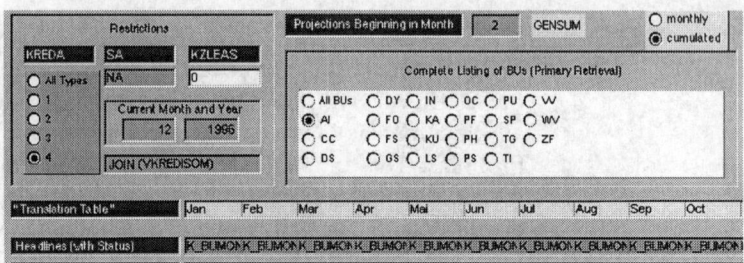

Exhibit 41: inSight® Help Level Display

6.2.6

Adjustments, Expansions

An information system is constantly being adapted and expanded to meet changing reporting needs. Shortly after the system has been rolled out, users usually register numerous requests for new features and displays. These requests should be not be taken lightly: They are often critical to the success of the overall system, as they are the needs identified by intensive use of the system.

inSight® modules can be quickly and easily modified, without endangering the performance of other application or system components. The time needed to make application changes can often be measured in minutes.

No Major Format Changes

Drastic style or formatting changes should be avoided at this stage. They should be reserved for major system renovations and expansions.

6.2.7

Distributing the Program and Applications

inSight® can be installed on an application server as well as on a PC. Using an application server insures that all users are always working with the latest program and application versions.

Write Permission to the Server

If multiple application servers are used in a large corporate network (more than 100 servers), a problem could arise with regards to automatically updating the program and application versions. Write permission on these servers is usually restricted. Meetings and discussions with the server administrator don't always bring about desired changes or modifications. For example, many administrators insist on retaining a (in this situation) superfluous application server password. It is difficult to explain to users why they need different passwords for logging into the server and logging into the application, and why these passwords are changed on irregular time schedules. If the data processing department insists on instituting an inflexible security policy, hard-earned user acceptance can quickly disappear.

"Pseudo BLOB" In cases like this, or when no application server is available, it is a good idea to use a relational database to update programs and applications. Using "Pseudo BLOB" technology (see page 58), inSight® can store files in a central table, and access them in any application. To check how current a document is, a "counter" can be used. A "counter" is simply an identification number associated with a document, that is increased by one every time a new version of the document is saved. It is thus possible to check whether or not a document is current before the document is actually opened. If a newer version of the document is available in the relational database, the older document will automatically be replaced. The same process can be used to distribute updates of the inSight® program, with the help of the VERSION (INSIGHTTYPE) function. This technology makes it possible to insure that all users always have access to the most current program and application versions.

Unlike the ease with which communication and repository files can be switched, the way in which start-up sheets are handled is a bit more complicated. A good way to circumvent this problem is to create a user-specific "pre-start-up" sheet with its own connection and repository files. The only role of the individual start-up sheet is to check if a newer version of the general start-up sheet is available. The true application start-up sheet can then be defined using the SETSTARTDOCUMENT function.

Although this practice is commonly used in many companies today, the extra maintenance associated with it leaves much to be desired. This practice is particularly problematic when multiple inSight® applications are sitting on a single computer, and a single start-up sheet has been designed for launching the different applications. Additionally, there are increased installation issues that arise with this practice, because extra communication components (along with the inSight® application itself) must be installed on the PC.

There is yet another issue to consider when the system is running on the Windows NT platform. Since it is not possible to overwrite program files, it is not possible to automatically update program versions.

ActiveX Will Replace
"Pseudo BLOBs"

In the very near future, it is likely that Internet technologies like ActiveX from Microsoft will largely replace "Pseudo BLOBs" for tasks like updating programs and applications. Users will thus be able to access inSight® applications over an Internet browser. It will no longer be necessary to have inSight® installed on a PC or a file server. inSight® applications will be available via an HTML page on an HTTP server running under Windows NT.

The ActiveX technology makes it much easier to operate and use inSight® applications. With a SecurID card, it is possible to access applications (ignoring the security implications of such a connection) from outside the Intranet. The SecurID card (see page 110) serves two purposes: It checks the user's access privileges to the corporate Intranet, and oversees the retrieval of information from the data server.

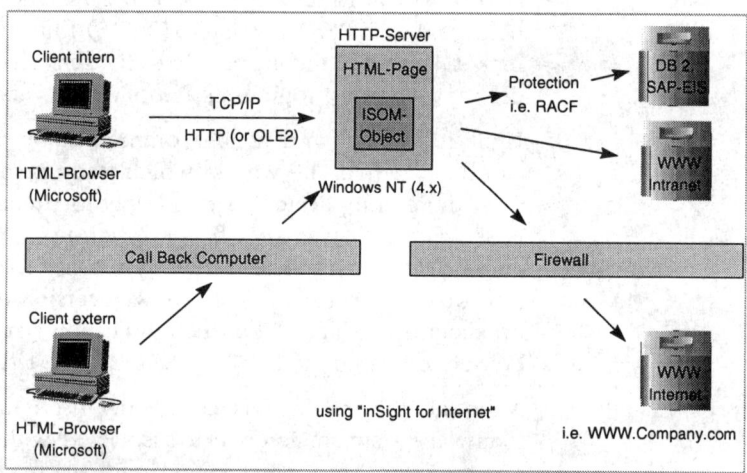

Exhibit 42: Intranet Access Using ActiveX Technology

6.2.8

Protection Classes

An information system contains data that needs to be protected against unauthorized access. Establishing different levels of protection classes is highly recommended. Not only is data restricted to those who need it and are authorized to use it, but protection classes also send clear signals about where the corporation places its information priorities.

Highest Protection in Class 1

- **Protection Class 1** data is the data that is so sensitive that even the system administrators are not allowed to see it. This includes transcripts from board meetings and personal data about high-level managers and executives. Ideally, the information in this class should be encrypted even before it is loaded into the server databases. The end user can only decode this data from a PC with a special "card reader" accessory; additionally, the user needs a personal card that is inserted into the   "card reader." Unfortunately, this type of data protection currently exists only in the form of a prototype.

SecurID Card

- **Protection Class 2** includes the data that the corporation deems too sensitive for general viewing. This class generally includes details about turnover and profit figures, but also includes strategic initiatives. The protection features of professional databases are recognized as being secure enough for this class of data. The problem of changing the password on a monthly basis (which most protection systems recommend) can be bypassed by using the so-called SecurID card (see page 110). The SecurID card uses a six figure number that is synchronized with the central system, and which changes every minute. The six digit number is used in place of a password. Experts agree that the security afforded by this system is also good enough for protecting external access to a corporate Intranet.

HTML Information

- **Protection Class 3** data is data that includes some editorial commentary or input. The system administrators are interested in restricting access to this data to certain groups of employees. This generally means the employees or departments who pay for the service in question. This class of information is often available in HTML form over the corporate Intranet. A good technological solution is to encrypt the data, and have an automatic data decoding process execute on the PCs of authorized users. This frees the system administrators from the complicated task of saving HTML information to a relational database. The system admini-strators must be sure to design the system in such a way that the users do not have to type in another password to access class 3 data. The data should automatically be available to authorized users after a general user identification has been entered.

6.3 Internal Marketing

6.3.1 Brand Name

ISOM

A corporate-wide information system needs a name that is both descriptive and memorable. A label like "MIS" (for Management Information System) fails to fulfill this purpose. The name can be traditional or progressive, depending on the culture of the corporation developing the system. In any case, the name must be easy to remember and to identify with the corporation. The goal for the brand name should be a name that the majority of the employees recognize, and with which they associate positive attributes, even if they know nothing about the system itself. An example is the name "ISOM" as an abbreviation for **I**nformation **S**ystem for **O**perative **M**anagement. This name is appearing in more and more memos and reports, often with the directive that certain data repositories should "absolutely be included in ISOM."

Brand Names Help Maintain Confidence in Rough Times

If the system is running without any technical or content-related problems, there is really no need for this type of support. But when problems arise (for whatever reasons), a recognized quality brand name can buy time for the system administrators to address the underlying source of trouble. A corporate-wide information system is constantly being evaluated by sponsors and users. It often takes years for a system to produce clearly recognizable tangible benefits for the firm. This presents additional challenges to system developers and information suppliers alike. In today's rapidly-changing business environment, and with the innovation explosions that are constantly rocking the data processing sector, it is easy to lose the initial goodwill and enthusiasm that a "new" information system generates. In this sense, internal marketing plans should be seen as a precautionary measure designed to insure support for the system in difficult times.

Preventing "Directional" Battles

Experience has shown that internal marketing plans also help convince employees that the new information distribution structure is both more efficient and more effective. General acceptance of the overall system concept is necessary to avert costly and time-consuming battles over the "direction" that the information system should take. Modest internal marketing costs are resources well-spent if they can prevent these debates from bogging down the system development process.

6.3.2   Logo

Developing a logo for the application can have positive implications for the overall acceptance of the application. The following picture shows the symbol for ISOM, the Information System for Operative Management.

Exhibit 43: ISOM Logo

Mousepad or Coffee Mug

There are numerous areas where a logo can be used to promote a new information system concept, like on mousepads or coffee mugs. These items can be given as rewards for "honorary" system helpers (from management, the technical departments, and data suppliers), and serve as a constant reminder of the system's existence.

6.3.3   User Handbook

A user handbook should always accompany an application, even with the most self-explanatory applications. Many people view a handbook as an essential part of the project "deliverable." It is important to insure that the optical appearance and overall layout of the handbook be on par with the actual displays and layouts in the information system itself.

Users are not the only employees interested in application handbooks. When a corporate information system was first introduced to 30 targeted end users, 250 handbooks were printed and completely distributed within days. Two revised handbooks were later produced, with 300 copies of each revision being distributed. A newer version of the handbook is currently in the works, and the planned number of copies to be printed, though not yet decided upon, is sure to exceed the 300. At the present time, the number of information system end users has been intentionally restricted to 300 users.

Best Publicity Builder

A handbook is unquestionably the best publicity builder for an information system. A handbook is seen as a prestige item, so it is important to steer copies of it to the people and departments where it will have the most impact. It is recommended that the latest version of the handbook be available in electronic form as an HTML document within the corporate Intranet, and that this electronic version be updated every time an addition or modification to the system is made. Of course, the electronic version may need to be modified to be compatible with and take advantage of HTML technology.

6.3.4   Information Catalog

An openly-accessible, summarized version of a catalog listing the ISOM theme contents is available to all system users. The real charm of the catalog is the ability to individually pick and choose selected theme areas which can be "ordered" online to create a personalized information system. The corresponding technical realization of a "personally-defined information system" is expected to take another year or two. The launching of an interactive information catalog should be preceded or accompanied by the corporate-wide integration of ActiveX or a similar technology (see page 180).

6.3.5   Creating a Hotline

The launching of an information system should be accompanied by the simultaneous introduction of a telephone hotline. A telephone extension should be manned during normal business hours, and be completely dedicated to fielding reports of technical disruptions and answering end user questions regarding the system contents. After-hours, the data processing desk should be available to record reported problems.

One Hour Response Times

The issue of acceptable hotline response times becomes a critical issue when the system in question is being used by board members of a global corporation. An external service that guarantees a response within one hour's time will add to the overall system costs, but the added cost is worth it if the corporate networks are unreliable or subject to constant disruptions. With stable networks and a stable data server, having a back-up PC (fully loaded and ready to run the MIS applications) has proven to be an effective solution.

6.4 Further Development

6.4.1 Expansions, Improvements

Looking at a three year old MIS application, it is apparent how quickly "cutting edge" applications can become outdated. On the one side, the demands and expectations of the end users have become more sophisticated. On the other side, new technologies and system development experience are available to system designers. It is only logical to assume that this trend will continue in the future.

Continuous
Development

Whereas older applications used new inSight® documents for new data display layouts, today it is possible to combine multiple display layouts in a single document. This is done through the use of buttons that switch different groups of object from visible to invisible and vice-versa, depending on the display selection made by the user. As a result, the total number of documents within an application can be substantially reduced. A standardized format for the sort function (see page 119) has also been developed. The practice of storing frequently-used formulas in function buttons (see page 66) has increased overall application clarity for both developers and users. Another trend is the increased use of local database functions. It is much easier (and faster and cheaper) to use data blocks stored in the main memory of a PC to access specific data records and to perform operations like display sorts.

Performance
Improvement

Some inSight® functions have been improved in later program releases. As examples, it is now possible to color code column or table entries based on the data contained in these objects, and to use the hierarchy conversion feature to reverse dependencies between menu objects (see page 122). The main reason for revising existing documents, however, is to take advantage of new functions and technologies that allow for overall performance improvements (i.e. improved response times). As a general rule, every document should receive a "face lift" every two to three years. The work this entails can usually be completed in a matter of hours.

6.4.2 Development of New inSight® Functions

New inSight® versions are released approximately twice a year. New functions are added to these versions based on user demands and developing technologies. Recent additions include the ability to access OLE objects and formatted texts stored in a relational database. Before a new function is added to inSight®, extensive testing is done to assure that the function works as planned, and doesn't conflict with existing functions. From this commitment to customer needs and the goal of staying on the cutting edge of technological advances, inSight® continues to evolve as a major player in the information system software industry.

6.4.3 Information Acquisition

Very few firms find themselves in a situation where theme area data already exists in presentation form, so that the company can simply build a display application for the data. Most companies face a much stiffer challenge. The root of this problem is rarely a lack of effort on the part of individual departments to provide data to the information system. The problem usually stems from the fact that the data provided is incomplete or of poor quality. Poor quality data in this instance refers to the structure of the data records as well as the actual contents of the data.

The first order of business is therefore a discussion with personnel from the areas delivering the data for the information system, to agree on a dimensions-hierarchy diagram (see pages 14 and 171) and to define the actual contents required by the system. A data usefulness analysis can then be performed to quickly evaluate how close the information system is to being ready for distribution. The ensuing data availability analysis often leads to a list of tasks that can easily require two years or more to accomplish. For the customers of an MIS, this time frame is incomprehensible and, even with extensive discussions and explanation attempts, unacceptable. For these reasons, an experienced information system administrator will continuously have multiple information acquisition projects in motion, so that new theme area modules are available for release every three months or so.

6.4.4 MIS Market Observations

Numerous discussions with software developers and consumers have confirmed that it would be difficult (if not impossible) to use other software programs to create applications similar to existing inSight® applications, at a comparable monetary or time investment level. This does not mean that there will never be a comparable software program. IT professionals, along with IT system users, need to continuously monitor developments in the market. The best benchmarks for new products and innovations are applications and programs with long, successful track records.

Long-Term Considerations

But even when a software tool that can fulfill present-day corporate reporting requirements (like inSight®) is found, there is no guarantee that the product will be able to meet the long-term needs of system users. User expectations grow as their familiarity with the system grows. If the software is not able to grow along with user expectations, the future success (and credibility) of the MIS is at risk. This is exactly what happened with an actual MIS system based on the macControl II software product. Introduced in 1993, the system met or exceeded all the requirements laid out for it by the conceptual development team. As user demands for faster response times and expanded theme areas grew, the system was unable to accommodate them (see page 143). The same risks await inSight® as well, although the illustration below makes it clear that inSight® is still ahead of the overall information system technology curve.

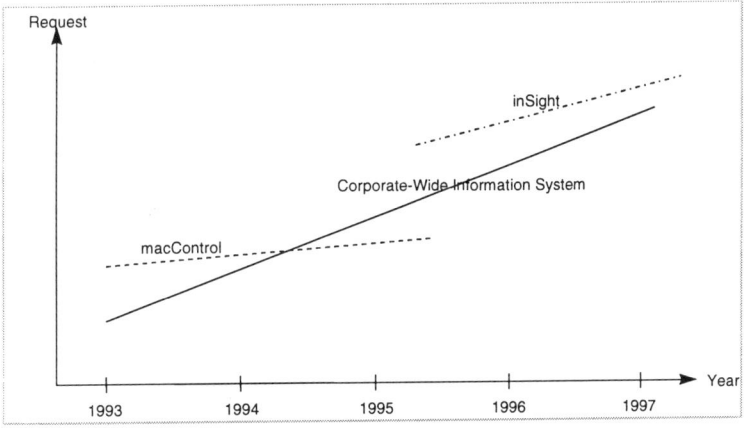

Exhibit 44: Software Capabilities and Expectations

A completely unrelated yet equally as important market observation tool has recently emerged. The Internet offers worldwide access to information. Much can be learned by observing the interfaces and layouts used by professional

Internet site developers. This is an especially valuable resource for areas incorporating unstructured information like formatted texts, etc.

6.5 Data Access Costs

There is no simple answer to the question, "How much and what type of access should an employee have to corporate data?" Answers range from "full access" to "no access," and often change based on the company's current priorities. As an example, if a company decides to run down its finished goods inventory, more employees will need access to information about inventory levels. Once the desired inventory level has been achieved, and the process of creating and shipping inventory has stabilized, detailed information related to inventory levels are less important to most employees.

Price

For this reason, it is advisable to avoid direct and ambiguous user surveys. Also, it is difficult to answer these questions without knowing the price of data access. When there are no data access costs, users tend to demand total access to all available data, even if they have no need for it.

Currently, if cost calculations are made at all, they are generally based on the number of times a system is accessed (or the amount of processing time needed for these accesses), or based on a single total system usage fee. Such a costing system is outdated, as it ignores the actual value of the individual pieces of information in the system. A modern information system concept should enable individual users to customize the system by selecting the theme areas that apply to their specific job tasks (and to which they have been granted access privileges). The user can simply log onto the system and select relevant theme areas from a list of available modules. Access costs are then calculated based on the specific theme areas (or modules) the user has selected (see page 144). The price charged for a theme area should reflect the data gathering and processing costs, as well as the costs associated with formatting the data in an attractive presentation form. These costs should be reasonably realistic and affordable, in order to strengthen (rather than weaken) the relationship between the data providers and the data users.

Subscribing to an
Entire Theme Area

It is not a good idea to charge a fee for every single data access. Like a newspaper, user's should be able to subscribe to entire theme areas, which can then be accessed as often as the user desires. Such a system also reduces the amount of print jobs run by users, as they are freed from worrying about the costs they incur every time they access the system.

User Attitudes
Change

An interesting problem surfaces when designated system end users are also members of the project oversight committee. Their primary interest in the system is to insure that it is simple, inexpensive, and that it accomplishes specific important corporate tasks. There is nothing wrong with emphasizing these system qualities. Problems arise, however, when the same people are judging the system from an end user perspective. Suddenly, the emphasis is on optically-pleasing displays, extensive data display possibilities, and a luxurious system interface.

6.6   Monitoring Success

How can the success of a corporate-wide information system be measured? Should the judgment regarding a system's usefulness be based on the number of active system users, or maybe the total number of times a system is used?

The Number of
System Accesses is
not Important

If the board of directors is selected as the user group for the system, that automatically rules out the realistic possibility of ongoing system acceptance and usage surveys. Besides, it is not important how often the system is accessed, but rather how convinced the users are that they system development is going in the right direction.

It is almost impossible to measure whether or not an information system improves the bottom line profit figures for a corporation. One is constantly confronted with articles proclaiming the spectacular successes of various information system projects, but the politics and spin control associated with these projects allows for a reasonable amount of skepticism as to the systems' true costs and benefits. What can be measured, however, is the savings a company reaps when they switch to electronic reporting over paper reporting. What has to be kept in mind with this comparison is the fact that the paper reporting system is one that has been optimized and refined over the course of several decades. In the early phases of introducing an information system, the traditional paper reporting system may appear to be more reliable and cheaper. To be considered successful, the long-term benefits of and savings from the information system need to be emphasized. Care must be taken not to use too many technical "tricks" and "gadgets," as this can easily scare employees into resisting the system.

Professionalism

If the system is to be effective and widely-accepted, a great deal of effort must be put into convincing the users of the system's overall corporate value. The contents and technical delivery of the product must always promote a sense of total system professionalism. Any and all system shortcomings need to be quickly identified and corrected. Unfortunately, many users are reluctant to complain directly to the system administrators, choosing to air their real grievances to an uninvolved third party. Recognizing this fact is a crucial step towards building a meaningful and productive dialogue between system users and system administrators.

The only reliable procedure for monitoring the true success of an information system is a variation of the "pay-per-use" system mentioned earlier in this book. This system forces the users to evaluate their information needs, and to evaluate the effectiveness of the various business models they choose to access. If a module proves unreliable or becomes irrelevant, the users will simply stop subscribing to it. If a particular module is losing subscribers, and efforts to make the theme area of that module more appealing to the users have failed, serious thought should be given to completely removing that module from the system.

A "pay-per-use" system puts a great deal of pressure on an information system and the system developers. Upper management should allow for a "honeymoon" period so the initial kinks and bugs can be worked out of the system, but at some point the system needs to prove its value to the corporation.

6.7 Corporate Newspaper

In the long-term, MIS applications will evolve in the direction of virtual newspapers, presenting the most important information on the start-up sheet. When a user clicks on one of the "headlines," detailed information on that subject will appear, along with the possibility to access additional related data. It is easy to imagine that a corporation could have any number of different virtual newspapers that all access the same base data, but provide different subscribing user groups with different headlines theme area emphases.

"OLINDA"

Such a system is technically possible today, albeit at a significant cost. It requires a combination of the **OL**AP, **IN**ternet and **DA**ta Warehouse ("OLINDA") technologies. The real problem, however, is the lack of professional support from an editorial perspective. The people responsible for distributing internal corporate information are unfamiliar and uncomfortable with these new media forms. And the "techies" within the company lack the necessary editorial skills to assume responsibility for selecting the information (and the information form) that is to be distributed. What is needed is an OLINDA editor, whose work is supported by (still to be developed) data processing tools.

From an organizational perspective, a central editorial unit for corporate information could be structured like in the exhibit shown on page 154.

Information Pricing

A classical MIS fits quite well into this concept. The central corporate editorial unit has responsibilities similar to those of a traditional information broker (see page 7). The biggest difference is the fact that, in addition to offering external information, central unit also supplies users with internal corporate information.

7

Summary

7.1 Basic Principles

The most important lessons and observations gleaned from building and maintaining corporate-wide management information systems (MIS) can be summarized into the following points:

- Basic principle: The MIS user should notice nothing about the system except for the user interface. All navigation and function executions need to be self-explanatory, and controllable with simple mouse clicks. **User-friendliness** is the most important success factor. To meet this demand, advanced interface programs like **inSight®** (from arcplan) are needed. Programs like MS Excel® are equipped with powerful data manipulation functions, but they are more complicated to use and are designed more for controllers and analysts than for MIS users (see page 52).
- **Desired changes** need to be implemented quickly. The system should be dynamic and "alive," not static.
- **Internal marketing** is very important. It is a good idea to create a descriptive name and distinctive logo for the information system (see page 182).
- A **modular concept** (both in a technical and organizational sense) is highly recommended. This does not mean that the existing information structures need to be replaced. The MIS is thus "only the technical platform," used to display the outputs of the various corporate data suppliers (see page 144).
- Instead of having an MIS "sponsor," it is better to have two **board members** responsible for monitoring the MIS development (see page 68).
- The idea of **placing the MIS operating team under the direction of the data processing department for a limited period of time** has proven to be a successful one. Such an MIS development group could consist of two controllers, a database specialist, and an application developer (see page 106).

- An end user "**survey**" should **not be undertaken**. Instead, it is advantageous to instigate intensive discussions with the controllers, analysts, and executive assistants who will be responsible for maintaining and explaining the various MIS modules in the system (see page 80).
- The customary **system requirements** are **not** needed. The MIS presents a variety of "offerings" (see page 172) from which the end users can choose.
- It can be advantageous to **incorporate** the **secretaries** of high-ranking system users into the information system development process. When any problems arise, they are likely to be their bosses' first stop (see page 140).
- Particular attention should be paid to insuring that the MIS is tied into the company's **data processing technical infrastructure** (see page 28).
- When data is prepared in the form of relational tables, **separate MIS tables** should be designed. These can be views or copies of existing tables (see page 94).
- The medium-range goal should be to retrieve system data from existing **SAP®-EIS** Reports (see page 48).

8 Appendix

8.1 Index of Exhibits

8.2   Glossary

Accounting System	Cost measurement system. A method used to determine the costs and resource of a corporation or entity within a corporation.
ALE	Application Link Enabling. SAP interface for real-time data retrievals from operative systems to SAP expert information systems.
Alias	An alternative name for a data source column, like using the term "Region" instead of the otherwise ambiguous column title "DR02".
arcplan	Düsseldorf, Germany-based software developer. Developer and vendor of inSight®.
ActiveX	Microsoft's product designed to compete with Java.
Aspect	Data entity generated by SAP®-EIS, which formats data into a useful business structure.
BLOB	Binary Large Object. Database storage unit for contents consisting of numerous characters, like formatted texts, coded pictures, or entire files.
Business Information Shop	Expanded version of a Data Warehouse.
Business Information Warehouse concepts	New SAP term for unifying diverse corporate information and resources (Open Information Warehouse and SAP®-EIS).
CfRoI	Cash flow Return on Investment. An important ratio for controlling operative results.
Client PC	A PC with specialized software capable of accessing centrally-stored data and programs over a network.
Client-Server Architecture	A system construction characterized by a server (containing central data and data processing programs), and client PCs equipped with software which enable end users to access the central data.
COBOL	COmmon Business Oriented Language. A high-level programming language for the business programming environment.
Customizing	Modifying standard software to meet the desires of customers.
Data Mart	Intentionally-designed redundant portion of a Data Warehouse.
Data Mining	Automatic identification of noteworthy trends or variations in large data repositories.

Data Warehouse	Database(s) with specially-prepared data for EIS applications, as well as the data acquisition and maintenance systems associated with the database.
Data Model	Often a component of the system requirements. An attempt to diagram the relationships between the various terms (entity types) or their contents (attributes) used in the system, and how they are and will be used in the information system.
DB2 Database	IBM's relational database system for mainframes.
Decision Support System	Information system for upper management
Development Systems	"Finishing" systems. Systems that periodically process data according to strict guidelines, and display the results in a standard display which the user is unable to affect.
Dimensions	Organizational classifications like Time, Region and Product Group. In this case, Country and Product would not be considered additional dimensions, but rather lower hierarchical levels of the Region and Product Group dimensions.
Drill-Down	Process used to navigate from one data display level to a more detailed level of data.
DSS	Decision Support System, see EUS.
DWH	See Data Warehouse.
EIS	Executive Information System.
Entity Relationship	The Entity Relationship model is based on the belief that the system to be modeled can be described in terms of different objects (entities) and their relationships to each other.
Expert Information Systems	Information systems designed to provide specific functional information and analyses, like for finance or marketing.
FIS	Finance Information System.
GUI	Graphical User Interface. Allows users to graphically interact with data, as opposed to using a symbol-oriented system.
Hierarchies	Levels of a dimension, like department, business unit, and corporation.
HTML	Hyper Text Markup Language. The popular programming language used to build pages on the WWW.
Hyper Cube	Specially-saved data units in the SAP system. The term "cube" is used to suggest how easy it is to view the data from any dimension.

Hyperlink	HTML language element. A cross-reference for additional information on the WWW; By clicking on the cross-reference, the additional information can be directly called to the user's screen. A cross-reference can appear as highlighted text or as a graphic symbol.
IMS Database	IBM's hierarchical database system for mainframes.
Index	Table of contents for a table that speeds the process of finding certain data sets (rows) in that table, so the system response time is better.
Information Broker	Information "dealer". In larger corporations, this term is generally used to describe the person responsible for system data acquisition.
inSight®	MIS Tool from the Düsseldorf-based company arcplan.
Internet	World-wide open computer network with no central administering body.
Intranet	A corporate-internal network that uses Internet programs and protocols.
Java	A new object-oriented programming language developed by SUN specifically for Internet usage.
Java beans	Java variation offered by IBM.
System Requirements	Detailed list of user needs for a proposed data processing system.
Legacy Systems	Older mainframe systems.
Legal Entities	In this text, refers to corporate entities
Link	see Hyperlink.
LIS	Logistics Information System.
MIS	Management Information System.
Meta Data	Data that describes the contents and relationships of database contents (data about data).
MS Access®	PC database from Microsoft.
MS Excel®	Spreadsheet program from Microsoft.
MS Word®	Text processing program from Microsoft.
Multidimensional Data Cube	see Hyper Cube.
Navigation	Moving from one data perspective to another within an information system.

Normalizing	A process in the relational theory intended to prevent data redundancies. Based on functional dependencies, attributes can be removed from a large table and stored in a smaller table. According to the degree to which redundancies have been removed, a relational database can be said to have anywhere from the first to fifth normal form (NF).
Object Orientation	1. In technical programming: The building of a source code through the use of functional objects as instances of classes. Other classes can then be derived from these objects (inheritance and multiple inheritance).
	2. In inSight® development: The elements which, when combined, constitute an inSight® document.
Open DWH	A Data Warehouse in which every user is able to formulate queries with whatever query tool they choose.
OIS	Operative Information System.
OLAP	Online Analytical Processing. An analysis procedure based on on-line processing.
OLINDA	A combination of OLap, INternet and DAta warehouse.
Online	The direct accessing of a data source by a dialog program, enabled by a network connection.
Open Information Warehouse	SAP term. The OIW directly accesses logistical data.
Operative Systems	Systems that process daily raw data, process the data, then make it available to individuals or corporate information systems.
System Specifications	A document compiled by the programming department. Defines the technical details of a system.
Proprietary	Restricted to the software and support of a single product vendor.
Pseudo BLOB	A BLOBs consisting of several combined BLOBs.
Pull Process	Data is fed into a system according to periodic automatic data copy actions.
Push Process	Real-time data retrieval, where data is automatically written to the system as it becomes available.
Query Tool	Query program for pulling back data from a database.
RAD-Tools	RAD = Rapid Application Development. Programs that promise fast system programming.

RCF	Remote Function Call. Technology used by inSight® to directly access (already processed) SAP®-EIS data.
Ad Hoc Analysis Tool	Help program that aids developers in finding structures and relationships.
Relational Database	A database that stores data in a two-dimensional table form, and can be accessed using the SQL query language.
Repository	Meta data library.
Road Map	Display mapping out which data sources provide what data content to specific display documents.
ROLAP	OLAP, supported by relational databases.
Runtime Version	In contrast to the developer version, which can be used to create new applications, the runtime version can only operate applications that already exist on the client PC.
SAP	A large German software developer.
SAP®-EIS	SAP's Executive Information System.
SAP® R/2	The older, mainframe-based operative SAP system.
SAP® R/3	The new operative SAP system with a client/server architecture.
Shareholder Value Concept	The idea that a corporation's most important "product" is the stock of that corporation.
SIS	Strategic Information System; identical to an MIS.
SQL	Structured Query Language.
Structured Data/Information	Data/Information in table form.
Styleguide	Guideline for uniform application formatting.
SVGA	Super Video Graphic Adapter.
TCP/IP	Transmission Control Protocol / Internet Protocol.
Unstructured Data/Information	Data/Information not stored in table form.
Pre-System	System that pre-processes data and is commonly used between an OIS and an MIS.
VTAM	Data storage system from IBM.
WWW	World Wide Web.

8.3 Index

8.4   Bibliography

[1]   ECKERSON, WAYNE: Red Brick Systems enhances its data warehouse product, in: Network World, Vol. 10, Iss. 25 (June 21 1993), Page 35

[2]   BEHME, WOLFGANG: Das Data Warehouse-Konzept, MUCKSCH, HARRY; BEHME, WOLFGANG (Hrsg.): Gabler-Verlag, Wiesbaden (1996), Page 35

[3]   HABERLAND, K.H.: Zur Planung automatisierter Management-Informationssysteme, in Koller, H.; Kicherer, H.P. (Hrsg.): Probleme der Unternehmensführung, München 1971, Page 102

[4]   HEINZELBECKER, KLAUS: Ausbaustufen eines EDV-Informationssystems, in: io-Management-Zeitschrift Industrielle Organisation, Vol. 47 (1978), Page 403

[5]   MEYER, B.: Lexikon der Informatik und Datenverarbeitung, SCHNEIDER, HANS-JOACHIM (Hrsg.), 2. Edition, München - Wien (1986), Page 290

[6]   BULLINGER (Hrsg.), KOLL, NIEMEIER: Führungs-Informationssysteme (FIS), FBO-Verlag Baden-Baden (1993), Page 19

[7]   MERTENS, PETER; GRIESE, JOACHIM: Integrierte Informationsverarbeitung 1 - Planungs- und Kontrollsysteme in der Industrie, 6. Edition, Wiesbaden (1991), Page 43

[8]   SCHEER, AUGUST-WILHELM: Wirtschaftsinformatik - Informationssysteme im Industriebetrieb, 3. Edition, Berlin et. al., (1990), Page 6

[9]   MERTENS, PETER; GRIESE, JOACHIM: Integrierte Informationsverarbeitung 1 - Planungs- und Kontrollsysteme in der Industrie, 6. Edition, Wiesbaden (1991), Page 5

[10]   SCHEER, AUGUST-WILHELM: Wirtschaftsinformatik - Informationssysteme im Industriebetrieb, 3. Edition, Berlin et. al., (1990), Page 402

[11]   MERTENS, PETER; GRIESE, JOACHIM: Integrierte Informationsverarbeitung 1 - Planungs- und Kontrollsysteme in der Industrie, 6. Edition, Wiesbaden (1991), Page 1

[12]   MERTENS, PETER; GRIESE, JOACHIM: Integrierte Infor-mationsverarbeitung 1 - Planungs- und Kontrollsysteme in der Industrie, 6. Edition, Wiesbaden (1991), Page 10

[13]   CONHAIM, WALLYS W.: Introduce yourself to an infor-mation professional, in: Link-Up, Vol 10, Iss. 6 (November/Dezember 1993) Page 10-11

[14]   Pilot Software – OLAP White Paper, in: http://www. Pilotsw.com/olap/olap.htm, June 1998, Page 1

[15]   CODD, E.F.; CODD, S.B.; SALLY, C.T.: Providing OPAP (On-Line Analytical Processing) to User-Analysts: An IT Mandat, E.F.Codd & Associates, White Paper (1993), Page 5

[16]   CHAMONIE, PETER: Das Data Warehouse-Konzept, MUCKSCH, HARRY; BEHME, WOLFGANG (Hrsg.): Gabler-Verlag, Wiesbaden (1996), Page 49

[17]   BISSANTZ, NICOLAS; KÜPPERS, BERTRAM: PC Magazin Nr. 34 (21. August 1996), Pages 36 - 38

[18]   WENZEL, PAUL: Betriebswirtschaftliche Anwendungen des integrierten Systems SAP® R/3, 2. Edition, Vieweg-Verlag Braunschweig/Wiesbaden (1996), Page 6

Effiziente Softwareentwicklung mit DB2/MVS

Organisatorische und technische Maßnahmen zur Optimierung der Performance

von Jürgen Glag.

1996. IX, 137 S. (Zielorientiertes Software-Development; hrsg. von Fedtke, Stephen) Geb. DM 148,00
ISBN 3-528-05363-1

Aus dem Inhalt :
Performanceprobleme: Symptome, Ursachen und Maßnahmen - Organisatorische Maßnahmen in der Softwareentwicklung - Fallstudien - Tuning - Checklisten

Das Buch von Glag zeigt, wie professionelle und effiziente DB-Anwendungsentwicklung im DB2-Großrechnerbereich und Client/Server-Umfeld sichergestellt werden können.
Der Vorzug des Buches ist es, daß sowohl die technischen Aspekte (Performance, Tuning) als auch organisatorische Maßnahmen zur Optimierung (wirtschaftliche Performance) dargestellt werden. Damit eignet sich das Buch insbesondere für den Einsatz in Unternehmen, die DB2 kostengünstig und sicher einsetzen wollen.

Abraham-Lincoln-Str. 46,
Postfach 1547,
65005 Wiesbaden
Fax: (06 11) 78 78-4 00,
http://www.vieweg.de

Änderungen vorbehalten. Stand September1998.
Erhältlich im Buchhandel oder beim Verlag.

vieweg

Information als
Wettbewerbsfaktor

Die Popularität des Data Warehouse- Konzepts unterstreicht die Notwendigkeit einer besseren Informationsbasis für Entscheidungsträger aller Managementebenen. Für die dritte Auflage wurde „Das Data Warehouse-Konzept" erneut in Teilen überarbeitet. Ausgehend von der Architektur sowie den charakteristischen Komponenten und Funktionen eines Data Warehouses analysieren namhafte Experten aus Wissenschaft und Praxis u. a. folgende Aspekte der Data Warehouse-Thematik:

- Fragen der Entwicklung,
- Datenmodellierung und -speicherung sowie die Eignung verschiedener Datenbankmodelle,
- rechtliche Aspekte und Datenschutz,
- Analysewerkzeuge und -techniken (OLAP, Data Mining).

Inhalt

Herausgeber Dr. Harry Mucksch ist Geschäftsführer der Servicezentrum INFOKOM GmbH in Papenburg. Dr. Wolfgang Behme ist Projektleiter im debis Systemhaus, Geschäftsstelle Führungsinformationssysteme, in Düsseldorf.

**HARRY MUCKSCH
WOLFGANG BEHME (HRSG.)**

**Das
Data-Warehouse-
Konzept**

Architektur - Datenmodelle -
Anwendungen
Mit Erfahrungsberichten

3., überarb. Auflage

GABLER

Harry Mucksch /
Wolfgang Behme (Hrsg.)
**Das Data
Warehouse-Konzept**
Architektur- und Daten-
modelle-Anwendungen.
Mit Erfahrungsberichten
3., überarbeitete Auflage
1998. XVI, 679 Seiten.
Broschiert ca. 138,00 DM
ISBN 3-409-32216-7

Erhältlich im Buchhandel
oder beim Verlag.
Änderungen vorbehalten.
Stand: Februar 1998.

Abraham-Lincoln-Str. 46 · Postfach 15 47 · D - 65005 Wiesbaden · Fax: (06 11) 78 78 - 4 00   **GABLER**